spiritually sassy

spiritually sassy

8
Radical Steps to Activate Your Innate Superpowers

Sah D'Simone

sounds true
BOULDER, COLORADO

Sounds True
Boulder, CO 80306

Published 2020

Cover design by Rachael Murray
Book design by Meredith March

Printed in Canada

Library of Congress Cataloging-in-Publication Data

Names: D'Simone, Sah, author.
Title: Spiritually sassy : 8 radical steps to activate your innate
    superpowers / Sah D'Simone.
Description: Boulder : Sounds True, 2020. | Includes
    bibliographical references.
Identifiers: LCCN 2019058217 (print) | LCCN 2019058218 (ebook)
    | ISBN 9781683644897 (hardback) | ISBN 9781683644903 (ebook)
Subjects: LCSH: Psychic ability. | Extrasensory perception.
Classification: LCC BF1031 .D75 2020 (print) | LCC BF1031
    (ebook) | DDC 204/.4—dc23
LC record available at https://lccn.loc.gov/2019058217
LC ebook record available at https://lccn.loc.gov/2019058218

10 9 8 7 6 5 4 3 2 1

Also by Sah D'Simone

5-Minute Daily Meditations

For my mom and dad

Contents

Introduction

Hello, my love. Welcome to *Spiritually Sassy*.

Spiritually Sassy distills the art of living well in our modern world in eight radical yet entirely attainable steps. The eight steps in this book lead directly to the heart. *Spiritually Sassy* is the *now* guide.

The steps in this book are not a quick fix. *Spiritually Sassy* is not some cute slogan for spiritual bypassing. It is an invitation to do the Work with a guy who's been there, with a guy you can relate to. A blend of Tantric Buddhism, evidence-based psychological knowledge, and my special sassy sauce, *Spiritually Sassy* is the modern answer to your suffering. You might be asking, "WTF do you mean by this big word, *suffering*?" I mean all of it: all the confusion you might have about who you are, all the past pains, the guilt, the shame, the hatred, the cruelties, the indifferences, the complacency, the list goes on—all the stuff that you might unintentionally be carrying with you and that is unfortunately running your life. It's a new approach to spirituality that wants you to start to heal your shit, reconnect with your heart, activate your innate superpowers, and make an impact in the world by being who you truly are. How shall I say this? *Spiritually Sassy* is about being your motherfucking self! I want you to remember how to be bold, to take up space, because deep down at the base of your being, you know all of it. It's time to remember, because the world needs your magic, your gifts. This is a new curriculum, and your homework is to be yourself fully by expressing your heart creatively.

I began seeking in a real way for something more when my life started to crumble. I was in my twenties then, a high-performing, anxious, depressed person working in the fashion industry as the cofounder of a successful magazine. I was living the life I thought I wanted, a life society told me I should have. I was making money, hanging out with celebrities, and I seemed to be successful. But I was deeply depressed, and I was starting to lose myself in drugs and alcohol. I was feeding my body crap, and I was completely out of tune with the real version of myself. What did I want? Who was I? And why, if I had everything I'd wanted, was I so damn unhappy? Who would I be without my social status? These questions were what drove me at first. As an immigrant in America, as a brown and queer individual, I had put a lot of emphasis on having stuff, and this had become my main vocabulary. As a result, everything I did was rooted in the drive to achieve a particular kind of success. This drive dictated the quality of my experience and my sense of self-worth. I was drawn to spiritual ideas, but I didn't know where to start, and I certainly didn't know how I could ever fit in with those circles. Where was my place, and what did I believe?

If you're like me, a linear path to inner freedom doesn't work. The path I needed was intersectional. It was not this or that, but everything in between, because I don't fit neatly inside any box. The definitions of spiritual life I saw around me didn't fit me, so I began to search for spaces that felt like home. Eventually I created the spiritually sassy way. I found home for me, and I want to invite you to it. Everyone is welcome here.

My search has led me all over the world. It led me to leave fashion and find a very different path in teaching, learning, and working every day to free myself. It led me to sit with and learn from spiritual masters, neuroscientists, contemplative psychologists, trauma experts, and all the wild and amazing people I met along my travels. And it has led me to a way of living that is drawn from all of my studies but that feels like me. I want to share with you the steps I have developed with the hope that in trying some of these practices and reading about what has worked for me, you will feel more like you. It is my mission to help you come alive.

I call *Spiritually Sassy* a curriculum because you will learn how to redesign your life and, ultimately, graduate from old ways of feeling, thinking, and acting. You will be able to fully step into what's in your heart as a way of life instead of being trapped in the habits of your conditioned mind.

Your Work may be messy, loud, flamboyant, or fabulous. All of that is okay. All that's required is that you show up with your whole self, especially all the parts that you are not proud of. I had an awakening of my own that I'll describe more in later chapters, but the point is, the result was not me becoming silent or Zenned the fuck out. My version of spirituality is fierce and fun, as spirituality should be. I invite you to do you as fuck. This may sound selfish and not very spiritual, but let me assure you, it is the opposite. When you are truly you, you give others permission to do the same. Because we are all deeply interconnected. As you uncover your sassy heart, you impact everyone. You can't see it with your eyes, but the knowing that arises from your heart tells the whole truth. The more you transform your internal world, the more you can help others do the same, and the more you help others, the more your inner world is transformed—the spiritually sassy path is a sustainable, healing cycle. When you meet someone who is living in their full power, there's something so beautiful about it. We're immediately drawn to them, and we're in awe of how they carry themselves. You are that person. I will help you to remember this.

Take a moment right now to pause. Visualize yourself completely free. Visualize yourself completely liberated, with all the answers, all the support, living your dream. Just for a moment, visualize this. This glimpse is one example of how you can access the beautiful technology of the heart. Your heart wants you happy, my love. Be with the feeling. Know it is your birthright.

Now take a walk with me. I want to be your guide across the bridge to your heart.

Are you ready?

GLOSSARY

Before we begin this journey, I want to let you in on some of the key vocabulary used throughout the book, just so we're on the same page.

Bitch

Bitch, in the way I use it in this book, is totally removed from the traditional, offensive definition. It is genderless. When I use it, I am referring to myself in a sassy way. It's sort of a nickname for myself or someone else, almost as if I'm saying "me" or "you," but affectionately. It's important to recognize its negative connotation and that it can offend people, but in this book, I am taking the word back and mean it in a positive way.

Girl

Much like *bitch*, *girl* is how I often affectionately refer to myself and others. It is also not gendered. It does not literally mean girl. On the sassy meter, while *bitch* is a ten, *girl* is maybe a six. Both are sassy, but *girl* is slightly tamer, only because it's not a curse word.

Heart

I'm not talking about your thumping, physical heart when I use this word, though that is where this heart is located.

I am talking about the spiritual heart. I believe this heart holds our true essence and the deepest wisdom we'll ever know. If there were a spiritual goal, it would be to know this place in yourself, learn to access it. All the practices, theory, and wisdom in this book are centered around this, and my mission is to have you know your heart, or at the very least, start giving it more attention.

High Vision

Living in the high vision means you are in alignment with your purpose and heart. You are living a heart-led life, and you are taking care of yourself emotionally, spiritually, and physically. You are in balance.

Karma

I will talk a lot about karma and karmic seeds, and when I do, I'll use the metaphor of the garden, meaning the internal karmic garden of your mind. We come into this life with our canvas far from blank. One can say karma is like our genetic, biological predispositions passed down from our family tree, which is not to say we should blame our parents and ancestors for who we are. Although at some level that is real, I want to bring attention to karma as it was understood by the historical Buddha. This karma places no blame; instead, it gives us complete ownership over who we are. What I'm about to say next is not for you to drink as spiritual Kool-Aid. I want you just to take it as a hypothesis: What if our karmic dispositions are inherited from our very own past actions from previous lives, and what if they have a direct impact on our current life? They are shaping the current version of YOU (but the good news is, they don't have to anymore!).

I won't get too technical in this book about karma, but I invite you to think of it as a bunch of wholesome and unwholesome habits you have inherited. These tendencies are creating everything you experience: the good, the bad, the happy, and the sad. It is our work to bring our agency to this creative process: to understand it and to find tools to support us in not allowing that stuff to run our lives and make decisions for us. Your karmic garden is where you have the power to decide which seeds you want to nurture and grow from moment to moment.

Mega Boss

A mega boss is someone who is living their purpose, inspiring others, and bringing positivity wherever they go. On a basic level, it is someone who is honest with themself and doing the Work. They are on their path, they're doing their Work, and because of that they are in the groove of life, reaping the benefits of all the opportunities they are tuned into, big and small. It doesn't matter what profession they have; all that matters is that they love what they do. Love radiates from them.

Merit

Merit is directly related to karma. Merit actually helps to counteract unwholesome karma (or bad habits). Think of merit as spiritual money being added to your bank account to offset a negative balance. Some actions have higher merit than others. Cultivating merit can be done with your thoughts, speech, or actions. When you think, speak, and act kindly to yourself and to others, you are cultivating positive merit, you're watering beneficial seeds in the karmic garden of your mind, and you're weeding out the harmful seeds.

And at some point, those beneficial seeds will blossom into a happier, more relaxed version of you. Don't believe me? Try it for yourself!

1

Coming Out of the Spiritual Closet

Congratulations, my love. You have taken a step in the direction of your well-being, in the direction of your heart. I am honored to have your trust as I share with you what I know to be true about what it takes to heal and be happy. Your wellness requires all of you: a trained mind and body so that you can listen to your heart. I promise to be honest and vulnerable and to hold your hand as we walk across the bridge together. Are you ready to go on this journey together? Are you willing to do the work?

This will not be easy, but I promise it will be worth it. In fact, sometimes it might be fucking scary. But guess what? You are worth it. Take a vow now. Repeat after me: *I am worth it.*

In this chapter, I'll go over the eight steps of the *Spiritually Sassy* curriculum so you know what's to come. I'll share what my spiritual coming out looked like, and you will begin to map out your own unique way of coming out of the spiritual closet, because being spiritual for ten minutes in the morning won't cut it. You are a mega boss, honey! You are a living legend, and you can spiritualize everything.

A NEW KIND OF SPIRITUALITY

So, what the heck do I even mean by "spiritually sassy"? There are many paths to freedom; what's so interesting about the sassy path? *Spiritually Sassy* is the culmination of all of my studies, from the West to the East and back. This vocabulary is not Buddhist per se. Rather, it's my own interpretation of everything I've learned through my study of Tantric Buddhism and contemplative psychotherapy, and through being a total junkie of liberation. It is the wisdom that I live by and that has become my guiding force. My teachings in this book will digest all of the things I've learned through the Buddhist path, and I'll share them with you in a very accessible, revolutionary, and rebellious way. While this book uses some Buddhist principles, it is not a Buddhist book. In fact, I'm going against what some of my teachers are telling me. It's a rebellious act but it's what I know and what has worked for me.

It's no secret: I am queer as fuck, I am brown as fuck, I am long- and curly-haired as fuck, I am Brazilian as fuck, I laugh loud, I'm extra, I love to dance, I call everyone "my love," I will tell you I love you after meeting you just once. These are also real things about me: I used to be an addict, I had shame about my sexuality, I thought I was worthless, I was severely depressed and anxious, I thought no one would ever love me, I fed my body garbage. These things are also real: I'm Buddhist, I meditate every day, dancing is one way that I practice freedom, I have studied with spiritual masters around the world, I practice kindness and forgiveness of myself and others as part of my daily work, I am not perfect. All of these things are parts of me. *Spiritually Sassy* makes space for all of this, and goes beyond to discover what is underneath all of it, the truth of who you are—your sassy, awakened heart.

My love, there is a place for you in the world. You deserve to have the life you want. You deserve to heal the parts of you that are wounded. You deserve to know that you are not your mental clutter. You deserve to know your awakened heart; you are worthy of hearing its plans for you. No two people have the same path because no two people have had the same experiences. We each have different gifts we have come here to share. We each have different wounds we have come here to heal. I'm tired of teachers saying, "This is the only way . . . " There are many ways of being free. The beautiful differences in all of us are ones the spiritually sassy path honors. I want you to be different. I want you to be YOU. Full power, honey! Because the true and genuine expression of you (the you that emanates from your heart field) is what will set you free, my love.

THE *SPIRITUALLY SASSY* APPROACH

My approach is guided by two questions: How can YOU be better? And how can you share your gifts with the world? I'm no guru, but I do have a few tools. I may be one, *maybe* two steps ahead of you on the bridge, but we're walking over it together. My way is inclusive: it honors you exactly as you are. My way has respect for your innate wisdom. Who are you and what have you come to do? The beautiful thing is that *only you know*! I am the conduit, here merely to give you some tools to help you shine the way you were put on this earth to. I will help you along the way in a language you can understand.

The *Spiritually Sassy* way is not a passive journey. Just because I love you doesn't mean this is going to be easy. It requires your full participation. But don't be scared! I'm not going to ask you to be silent for thirty days or meditate for long periods of time (though don't get me wrong: you totally can if you want to! I'm not knocking it), or stop enjoying life, or wear all white, or get talked at for an hour (but if that's your thing, that's cool). The *Spiritually Sassy* way asks you to fully participate in your evolution. This is where the fun part comes in.

My teaching method is all about bringing fun and lightness—joy—back into spirituality. I am going to ask that you use your whole self in this process. Mind, body, and heart wisdom. I will ask you to move your body. I'm serious. You're going to dance and jump up and down at times. You're going to remember you have a body. Why? Because I believe, and science proves, that trauma is stored deep inside of us and movement gets it out of our system. Things will get messy, and you will whisper to yourself, "I feel like crap, but I'm OKAY!" We are going to play. Why? Because we are all creative beings. Creativity is so fucking spiritual. By the end of this, we are going to remember that we are creative, innately genius beings who have simply forgotten how to live from the heart field.

It's all about uncovering the part of you that is fully awake, the heart. The heart is the essence of anything remotely spiritual. The function of meditation, mindfulness, and the essential teachings of Buddhism are about leading with your best qualities, and your best qualities live in your heart. We suffer because we lead with the untrained and deeply conditioned mind and not with the heart. Period. Truly, I've got nothing to add. The Buddha said it all. His Holiness the Dalai Lama has said it all. The great teachers have said it all. What I *do* have is an approach that people can hear. All people. One that people can understand. As I said, I'm the conduit—the brown-bodied, queer, immigrant, flamboyant, joyous, dancing conduit—giving you a few tools so you can learn to train, pacify, and purify the mind to recognize your heart essence. It's not as easy as it sounds. But doesn't it sound oh so good? The eight steps in this book are an integrative approach that includes a modern twist on the steps to freedom the historical Buddha taught. Think of me as a sassy translator. The wisdom remains the same, but there is a new teacher in town. My steps, like I've said, are inspired by Buddhism and other modalities, but they're my own.

How *Spiritually Sassy* Is Different

The first time I went to India and Nepal, living in retreat centers and monasteries, I had become a very "serious" practitioner. When I say "serious," what I mean is that I lost my connection to joy. By intellectualizing spirituality, I was missing the point. The mind likes a story. Essentially what I was doing at that time was living out a story of what I thought ULTRA SPIRITUAL people do. These mega-spiritual people were very quiet, they ate very little, they didn't laugh loudly, they didn't move flamboyantly. To be frank, because these ashrams, dharma centers, and monasteries lacked diversity, I was looking to straight white men and imitating how they were living their spiritual path. But they were doing what was needed for *their* personal healing, not mine.

When I began to travel and meet Buddhist tantric masters, I stumbled upon a teaching style that had all of us in the audience laughing: the teachers were sassy. When they came out, it was a wonderful spectacle. There was so much to smell, to see, to experience. All of these sensory pleasures that normally distract us from our heart were taking me back to my heart, though I didn't know that then. I thought that these masters could do all of this because they were already fully awakened, that I couldn't possibly act the way they did. I thought I needed to continue on this very ascetic path—until I finally realized, through the help of these masters, that I'm more of a tantric than an ascetic practitioner. I have access to extreme emotions, I like beautiful things, I like to laugh and dance. In the tantric path all this, plus everything the modern world has to offer, can be used to help us uncover our hearts.

Later on, of course, I discovered that's what I'd been called to do. But early on, when I was living in Nepal and India, I was obsessed with these quiet practitioners who ate very little and dressed very simply. Even so, my edge still creeped in. I found myself putting on my drapes and trying to subtly style them. I would braid my hair at night so when I woke up at 4:45 am, my hair would be looking good and I'd have enough time to work out before going to the meditation hall. I even got called out in the meditation hall. Someone asked, "Who is jumping rope at five o'clock in the morning before doing prostrations?" Oops. "Hi, it was me." In those days I was starting to lose my sass by trying to be someone I wasn't. These ascetics were all about renouncing modern living because that was their path. But my path is tantric. Now I know that. I believe in using all the modern world has to offer to connect with joy and intention every moment and every day.

Finding myself on my spiritual path was not just a question of ascetic versus tantric. In the spiritual space, the narratives have been dominated predominantly by heteronormative, cisgender, white voices. As a young, brown millennial, I often felt isolated, the minority on many levels in these spaces. Where does a brown queer man from Brazil by way of New York City fit in? The spaces I knew of were not serving young people, people of color, people in urban settings, or millennials at large. I craved something new. My version of spirituality is not about talking at you and telling you how to live. I promise you'll never get that from me. I teach in a way that removes all the things that I didn't like about spirituality, the things that I didn't connect with, the things that weren't useful to me on my journey. The heart of my style of teaching is about creating environments that are accessible and inclusive for the world we live in: brown, black, queer, straight, femme, flamboyant, masculine, transgender—our modern world. The way I teach is very much about creating a safe space where there has traditionally not been one. This is the space I have been looking for and the space I know so many others are seeking.

I am here to let everyone know that spirituality doesn't equate with whiteness. I am here to bust up the absolute truths we've been fed. "We're all one," for example. While this is a beautiful truth, it doesn't translate very well in the modern world. In fact, we have many differences. *Spiritually Sassy* believes everyone is (some)one. And for all the lip service given to "oneness," society doesn't treat many of its citizens as though we're all one. Society tells many of us daily: you are different, you are bad, you are wrong, you are not worthy. Living in a world this unjust while blindly believing in oneness is at worst a lie, and at best a denial of how the world works in an everyday sense. Yeah okay, one love. But, bitch, I was depressed as fuck! Can your oneness get me out of bed? Oneness is not on my side when I walk into a room as the only brown and queer body, when before I open my mouth, ideas and assumptions about me—that have a real effect on my reality—are being nonverbally communicated. Oneness couldn't get me a new job or change my behaviors, either. This was my experience as an early seeker. I felt "othered" many times over as the only brown, queer person in spiritual spaces. I lacked both language and tools for my depression, my disconnection, and my sense of isolation. I wanted so badly to connect, but I felt the reality of my lived experience creeping into my practice. Oneness wasn't helping me. As the queer, immigrant, flamboyant, brown person, I *was* the different one. My whole life I had been.

I am certainly not suggesting that we dwell in duality, either. But I am suggesting that we need a more realistic and inclusive approach for modern life. Was I worthy? Did I belong? The answer eventually came. YES! That hard-won YES is what guides my teaching practice today, and my relatable, real, accessible approach is what guides *Spiritually Sassy*. I *am* different, and that is beautiful. I *am* different, and I am worthy. If oneness is for everyone, then *Spiritually Sassy* is spirituality for everyone else.

Spiritually Sassy is deeply personal to me. On my path, which I'll share throughout the book, I lost myself. I thought losing myself was a necessary part of the process. I'm not being funny here. In all seriousness, I thought not showering regularly, eating with my hands and only once a day, dressing in all white, being the quietest one . . . I thought *that* was being spiritual. I lost my sass during those years. What I didn't know was that my sass was an innate quality. It's one of the ways I reach people; it's one of the reasons I connect.

The Goal

The goal? Simple. Freedom, honey. Because we are done feeling like shit. It's time to get free, not high. The key to freedom? Awareness. We live our lives, especially today as we are more and more plugged in, completely unaware of our deepest selves. As a result, we react to life in ways that are totally out of whack, leaving us imbalanced in myriad ways. Trapped inside the nonstop feel-think-react circuit, we have absolutely no space to respond to life (emotions, relationships, ourselves) in any skillful way.

Spiritually Sassy, at its heart, is about creating space in our internal world to step back—before the narratives, choruses, and orchestras of our fear/shame stories start up and respond to life for us. These false stories are the reason for our suffering. Beyond these stories is freedom. The path is through the heart. Yet there is an invisible wall holding us hostage to our conditioned minds and keeping us away from the heart.

Freedom is a tall order, I know. You might have many questions at this point, like, *How can I be free? What does freedom look like? Is freedom really possible?* I believe that freedom means living a purposeful life. My students come to me for a couple of reasons: because therapy only went so far, and because they want purpose. Everyone is looking for someone else to give their life purpose because living a life of "shoulds" seems so much easier than dropping down and investigating our inner lives. But you can only "should" for so long. Freedom is much simpler than it may seem. To know your innate qualities of compassion, kindness, creativity, and wisdom (and use them) is to know freedom. Freedom is finding your deep inner fountain of stability that you can count on no matter what, and to use that inner fountain is Purpose.

Sure, we'll have glimpses of oneness. But maybe not every day. Maybe we *will* eventually arrive at oneness, but on the spiritual path, there is no goal; it's simply about uncovering what is already there. And maybe all we'll have are many glimpses, and that's okay. These glimpses add up; they are moments of freedom. That is real life in the real world. The freedom I'm talking about, though, is absolutely possible for every one of us, every day. The kind of freedom I'm talking about happens when we begin to clean up our act, when we learn to breathe, when we create space between the stimulus and the habituated responses, when we can sit for a little while each day, when we update our inner software a little bit at a time. Eventually, we touch base with our divine qualities—our heart.

࿊

Spiritually Sassy will transform your life in the following ways:

- The mind gets less sticky; with fewer worries about the past or fears about the future, you actually enjoy the present moment.

- The mind stops clinging, so life's highs and lows don't stick for too long.

- Your default mindset upgrades to happy, compassionate, wise, creative, abundant, and brave.

- You become proactive, not reactive.

- Crazy habits are tamed.

- Insatiable cravings are under control, and the body is energized.
- You recognize your essence.
- You start to hear your heart.
- You stop blaming yourself and being the victim.
- You make friends with change and accept the impermanence of everything.
- You realize everything is connected.
- You know your mission in the world.
- You easily live a life of purpose.
- Through your everyday actions, you inspire others.
- You become a sassy bitch!

THE EIGHT STEPS

Okay, my love, so the way I designed it, the steps are meant to be followed one after the other, because they build on each other. Each graduation adds to your awakening.

Step 1: Know your story to change your story.

We'll explore the mental habits and patterns that are keeping you stuck and learn about science-based ways to rewire yourself.

Step 2: Learn to forgive yourself and those motherfuckers who have hurt you.

We'll discover the power of forgiveness and gratitude as a direct path to liberation and a necessary one on your journey.

Step 3: Spray spiritual bleach on the belief systems that have kept you stuck.

We'll clear out the old ways of thinking and make room for a new story that reflects your fabulous heart, not your inner critic.

Step 4: Wake up your inner wisdom.

Here, we'll get real about what our dreams and goals are and then learn powerful manifestation practices to help make them happen.

Step 5: Name your superpower.

Here you'll discover your innate superpower or personal signature. You'll explore your talents and qualities and tap into all you have to offer in a deep way. You'll find out what your unique mission is.

Step 6: Believe you're amazing.

You'll learn to get out of your own way in a big way. We'll explore the reality of how the fear of succeeding could be holding you back unconsciously.

Step 7: Use what you have.

Here, you'll learn the importance of looking beyond yourself to your community, your tribe, and considering how you give back. Being of service is a sustainable path to liberation. You'll learn to use what you have to make an impact.

Step 8: Stay slaying.

This is the maintenance level. We'll learn how to develop emotional fitness routines and practices that support your continued evolution.

NOT A QUICK FIX

The biggest problem I see in people seeking spiritual transformation is the desperate need for it to happen quickly. But quick fixes merely rearrange internal chaos. They don't process it or move it out of your system. It's imperative that you take the spiritually sassy journey nice and slow. Why? Because it took a very long time to create the causes and conditions that support the experience you're having right now, so it's going to take some time to create new conditions that support a new experience.

The commitment I want you to make right now is that you'll see yourself through the end of the book and try out all the practices. I want you to commit to one single thing every day—your potential to be totally free. I want you to make time each day to remember that there is a part of you that is already completely awake. Don't be intimidated by the word "practice." Practice just means making time to remember your awaked nature.

The Sassy
Foundation

In this chapter we'll go over the foundations of the spiritually sassy path. If you're reading this book, there are some habits, behaviors, and patterns you want to change. But how do we begin the process of change? I want to be sure we're on the same page about you, and most importantly, your heart.

OWN ALL OF YOU

I feel so miserable. Why are shitty feelings my default? Ugh. Loneliness, low self-esteem, the effects of trauma, childhood wounds, depression, anxiety, low self-worth, rejection, self-loathing, addiction, triggers. We accumulate this stuff—responses to pain—as we go through life, thinking that our mental tricks and avoidance will keep us safe from more harm, but what we accumulate through experience is actually the least of it (not to freak you out).

We actually come into life with an internal garden filled with karmic seeds, virtuous and non-virtuous. With the "right" conditions they blossom as mental tendencies, which creates all habitual patterns, the ones that support our heart and the ones that keep us stuck in suffering.

As I've said before, take this as a hypothesis: from what the ancient Indians and what the historical Buddha observed, it is said that we share the same tendencies as our family members, and one can say we have chosen our family so they can help us see our minds and graduate from old harmful curriculums together, as well as cultivate our virtuous seeds, like creativity, compassion, wisdom, love, and joy.

Through the "right" conditions I mentioned earlier, your karmic garden is cultivated. So, if your parents were shouting or fighting or drinking or just not there, this early dynamic sprouted pre-existing karmic seeds that perpetuate suffering. And through a scientific perspective, the study of transgenerational epigenetics (which we'll talk more about later), you realize, "Oh my goodness! These tendencies have been in my family tree all along."

But don't freak out—it's not all bad! The beauty of knowing all this is that, as science proves, you can redesign your genetic makeup, you can change the architecture of your brain, you can upgrade your default mindset spiritually, and by doing so, you are wiping out your karmic garden of unvirtuous seeds that have been suffocating your virtuous ones.[1] You're shifting your vocabulary to that of the language of the heart rather than the language of internal chaos, and you're tuning into the frequency of the heart, beginning to let it support, nourish, and guide you on your path toward freedom.

You Are Good

I remember the first time in my journey I was told I was good. I was in the Himalayas taking a course with a Canadian Buddhist nun. She was talking about Buddha nature and how everyone is good at their essence. I was not at home in myself yet, still very disconnected, and when she spoke to the audience, I felt she was speaking directly to me. I started to cry because no one had ever looked me in the eyes and told me I was good. We are taught to believe we are bad, wrong, not good enough as soon as we have language and even sometimes before, through all kinds of negative nonverbal messages. I began to think, *What a fucking epidemic! Why aren't we being reminded regularly that we are good?*

No one is born bad. The truth is that we are all innately good, we are all innately mega boss, superstar, high-vision, awakened Buddhas. Our work is to release the blocks and veils that prevent us from seeing who we really are.

The Karmic Garden

I use the garden metaphor in this book and when I teach because botany, plant science, is a simple way to better understand the concept of karma. Karma, as you probably know, is traditionally about actions: our accumulated actions from past lives and the effects of those actions that got translated into this life. There's something useful about that concept, but it may be too abstract for many of us. So, I like to break it down to the idea of a garden. Imagine each of us has a garden in our mind. Ideas and beliefs, patterns and habits are the plants that grow in this garden. It is the job of each of us in this life to tend to our garden. What is the primary work of gardening? Weeding, planting new seeds, watering, and continuously nurturing the good and weeding out the harmful or unwanted.

Because this garden is made up of mental habits, the way we must tend to it is also through the power of the mind—through nurturing good intentions, zapping negative thoughts with positive ones, cultivating merit, wishing others well and helping people, understanding the patterns of the mind, introducing new neural pathways for healthier patterns and behaviors, and creating new habits. It's about nurturing those seeds and weeding the old patterns and habits and behaviors continuously. Old stuff will show itself as triggers and negative emotions and feelings that spark old behaviors. For example, every time I pass by someone smoking a cigarette, craving is triggered for me and I have to actively choose to weed out that thought right then and there and choose another. That's just old karma ripening. I don't have to pick that fruit. I can pick another, more skillful fruit that I've grown, and eventually, that old karma will quiet down and stop growing quite as big.

The beautiful thing about this karmic garden is that it's yours, and you can learn to be empowered and in control. You have the power. You are the gardener and the landscape architect. You get to decide the design of this garden and what you want to grow here for the rest of your life. Once we realize that each intention, thought, feeling, word, and action we have is nurturing either a beneficial seed or a harmful seed, we can see just how in control we are.

So, in your garden there are seeds that will set you free or seeds that will keep you stuck: it's that simple. What seeds are you watering? I bet that unknowingly, you have been nurturing some harmful seeds that have kept you in a cycle of unhappiness. That is about to end. You are about to go deep into your mind, and by the end of this book, you will have the ability to make far wiser choices moment to moment about how you want your garden to look and feel. You will have a much better understanding of what the weeds look like, what the weeds are attracted to and vice versa, and what the beautiful, healthy flowers and plants are that you want to grow even bigger.

I also want you to understand that there is no such thing as bad karma. There is just karma. Life is one big dance of light and dark. You just gotta learn to dance with it. We would not be our sassy selves if we didn't have a balance of both, but balance is key. When the harmful karma starts to dominate, that's when we feel out of control and need to take a look at the garden. Karma itself is sassy. It makes us who we are. We each have our own unique and beautiful stuff to work out. Your work makes you, you. We are all here to work it out, so there's no shame in it. Karma is the great equalizer; we all have it; we've all got shit, my friend. But will you be a spreader of positive seeds or negative ones?

Growing Your Spiritual Bank Account

I like to think of a Buddhist concept, merit, as spiritual money. It's directly related to karma. In addition to learning new, more skillful thoughts and behaviors, another powerful way to purify the mind and cultivate virtuous karma is through merit. Merit is something you accumulate, and one of the most powerful ways to accumulate merit is by being generous. Basically, when you help others, when you make someone feel good by offering a compliment, or you act altruistically, you send someone love and well wishes. These actions not only benefit them, but they also add up in your spiritual bank account and act as a fertilizer in your karmic garden. These actions pour water onto the positive seeds you've planted and encourage growth in your life and in the lives of others. Helping others and making others feel good is one of the most powerful things you can do spiritually.

In this book, I'm always going to say things like "for the highest good of all." That's because, again, nothing you do happens in a vacuum. You have a great effect on everyone you come into contact with. You're going to be doing a lot of self-work in this book, but I'm always going to return to the question, *How can you help others?* Everything we do on the spiritually sassy path must be for the highest good of all, not just yourself. We are interconnected. All of the gardens feed one another. When you help yourself, you help others. That is a big truth.

GETTING TO THE HEART OF YOU

What if I told you that your only job in this life was to live from your heart and express to the world your heart's mission through service, action, and love? No big deal, right? This is essentially what we mean by activating your innate superpowers, and this is the heart of the spiritually sassy approach.

Be you. You know who that is. Or do you? If I asked you who you were, you might say, "I'm Alex, I live in San Francisco, I'm a dog dad, I have two siblings, I'm an architect, I'm single." That's not the You we're talking about. That's the you that you show the world ("Hi, world, accept me, I'm normal, I'm okay"). I want you to go deeper. The You with a capital Y I'm talking about lives in your heart, my dear. Chances are, you need a little help getting through the weeds in your karmic garden, all the bullshit you've been taught, and all the bullshit that society has crammed down your throat to have any idea who or what that is. Chances are, behind the You you show the world, you're dealing with over-whelming thoughts of inadequacy, of imposter syndrome, of unworthiness, of low self-esteem, of regret, of negative self-talk, of anxiety, and depression. You name it. Don't feel bad—these are the skills we've been taught for deal-ing with life: pretend everything is okay, do what you have to do to survive and fit in, and cope with the feelings or push them down with addictions like drugs or alcohol, the Internet, food, porn, or toxic people. You name it. But now it's time to 1) find out who you are, and 2) learn healthy ways to support this version of you.

So, let's try this again. Honey, do you know who you are? Like, for real, for real? This is key. For all the shit going on inside you, around you, and in the world, what if I told you that there was a part of you that was always at peace, always free, always joyful, and that with practice, you could learn to access that part of you and trust it to be the default way you show up? The step that comes before the eight steps in this book involves discovering that self (like, hello, where the fuck have you been while I've been up here stressing and going through shit?!). The eight steps in this book are meant to help you build a life around that person. That is where I come in, where this book comes in.

If your life isn't quite matching up with who you know you are, with what you know deep inside to be your potential, you're not alone. Life is hard! Being human is hard! Being around other humans is hard! It's like a fucking obstacle course sometimes. And an emotional shit show—dealing with heartache and trying to manage our internal world while showing up in the world. It's no wonder we get lost or off course. It's no wonder we teach ourselves to hide. It's no wonder we avoid connection. We are just trying to protect ourselves, for fuck's sake. It can be scary out there!

All this talk about the heart and about the real you: it can all start to sound like more bullshit. You're probably like, "Who the fuck is this dude telling me I don't know who I am?" That's a natural response of the mind. Because of our conditioning, the untrained mind's default is judgment and meanness to ourselves and others, its default is to be skeptical and untrusting. It is fearful, paranoid, cruel, and it tries to protect you from embarrassment and failure by talking shit to you and being mean to you, convincing you not to take risks and then shaming you when you do. What a fucking downer. It's not *trying* to ruin your life, it's just how its old processing software operates. It's cracked the fuck out. It goes on and on and talks and talks and narrates and predicts the future and is usually pretty negative. How often is your mind like, "I'm so fucking awesome and I did a great job, everyone loves me"? More often, your mind is probably like, "I must have looked so stupid, I really fucked this one up. I hate myself. I'm a piece of shit. Fuck you." Am I right? Your mind is also brilliant, of course, don't get me wrong, but if your *neurotic* mind (the one that never shuts up) was a person, you would never wanna hang out with them! The mind is doing this, believe it or not, to keep you safe (we'll talk about this later in the book).

But your heart. Mmm. Just thinking about it makes me calmer. But it's important to understand that the mind and heart are indistinguishably one—they've just stopped communicating. If your untrained mind is the person you never wanna hang around, your awakened heart is your most nurturing, accepting, loving friend with a warm smile who is generous and kind and makes you feel like everything is okay. That friend lives in you, my dear. It lives in all of us. It's just that the mind can be so damn loud, we never hear the heart's invitation. It's whispering, "Hey, come hang with me, you're worthy of unconditional joy." But you can't hear it. So, at the heart (pun intended) of the spiritually sassy steps—the point of it all—is to move your attention away from the loud-ass neurotic mind and down into the base of your being, the heart. Freedom is waiting for you there.

WHAT WE TALK ABOUT WHEN
WE TALK ABOUT THE HEART

I want to come back to the heart. I know, I know, I know . . . I'm obsessed with the heart. But it's time for you to get deeper into this heart curriculum. When I talk about "the heart," let's get something straight. I am not talking about the romantic heart. The romantic heart is an aspect of the spiritual heart. And I do not mean the physical muscle pumping in our chest. According to Buddhist tantra, where the heart organ lives is the path to our spiritual heart, that knowing place within you where your essence lies.

This deep heart that I'm talking about is our natural state. In Buddhism, they call this natural state Buddha nature. It is our potential to be completely awake and to remember that we already are fully enlightened Buddhas. We just forgot. The language of the spiritual heart is supportive, it's compassionate, it's kind, it's courageous, it's creative. And the default of so much of our mind has been conditioned with pre-existing karmic seeds of insecurity, doubt, shame, and guilt.

When we're talking about the spiritual heart, it's best described—though it's very hard to describe it with words because it doesn't communicate in words—as a deep, inner knowing. It is not *I know*. It is *a knowing*. Notice the difference. Even the witness drops and just pure *knowing* arises.

Look into the heart as often as possible and allow the inner knowing to arise! This is what will permeate every area of your life. It will guide you in what you need to eat to create a healthier body. It will guide you in what you need to do to change your default mindset from having unsupportive, negative, unskillful thoughts and feelings to having supportive, skillful, compassionate impulses of the spiritual heart. It will guide you in what your purpose in the world is.

As humans we've been given the abilities to think and feel, and we've been given our senses—smell, sight, touch, taste, and hearing. These are tools that we have to help us recalibrate ourselves back into the heart. I believe the purpose of human life is to get into the heart so much that you become a broadcast of healing, of love—a compassion factory where you're also helping others to enter into a balanced and regulated state.

It's important to stop asking why because the WHY is the mind wanting to add things in a linear way. The whys are keeping us distracted from the hows. How do I live better? How do I get closer to the heart? How can I help others? How can I do better today? Instead of asking why, ask HOW. How is a heart-centered question.

The beautiful part about this work is that the further you get down the spiritual path and the more you're connected to the spiritual heart, the fewer questions there are. You're less questioning and more accepting. You begin to see harmony even in the most chaotic places. You recognize your innate ability to connect with the potential of even the most broken parts. And when you are more accepting of reality and the mysteries of life, that sense of acceptance permeates your whole being. That's when you know the spiritual work is working. You're not numbing out because you can't find answers. You have already

established a foundational knowing that resonates acceptance of everything. It's very different from our habitual
default mode, which is all about quantifying and adding
on layers and layers of *why mind, why heart, why this, why
me, why my life, why, why, why!* The inner knowing will
arise and the sense of acceptance will permeate, and this
will become your default.

This is totally possible. In fact, it's already here. When
you train the mind, you uncover your essence. Be open to
the mystery of life. If we knew all the answers for everything, life would be so boring. You'd be bored. I'd be bored.
I trust that more and more answers will arise out of my
life. And here's the beautiful thing: When there's a truth,
there's a full-body knowing. When the body is in a cali-
brated state, in a healing state, the mind is relaxed, and
when the heart speaks, you just know. Goosebumps don't
lie. Trust this communication.

THE LANGUAGE OF THE HEART

As I've said before, the mind and heart are indistinguishably one, yet they communicate very differently.[2] It might
be helpful to think of it like a chariot. The horses driving the
chariot are the senses, and the charioteer (a.k.a the mind) is
guiding the horses with all of its crazy neurotic tendencies
(karmic seeds, genetic predispositions), and inside the car-
riage is the heart. So, the untrained mind, supported by the
horsepower, is desire-oriented—it wants stuff, it constantly
wants to consume things to make it feel better. It can't
accept the changing nature of all things. It's insecure, so it
craves validation, attention, and distraction, but in the end,
all it is, is a longing for clarity and a-wakefulness, which
dwells in the heart. The heart, on the other hand, has needs
as opposed to desires. Needs are different from desires.
While desires lead us to short-term pleasures and quick
fixes, needs are things we cannot live without, especially

because each time a need is met, the way to a happy inner garden is paved. So your senses become trained and the mind becomes more heart based. Just as our physical body needs water, food, and sleep to live, the heart needs love, wisdom, compassion, and joy—each of these qualities will support you to see yourself and the world in a different way, each serving a different purpose yet inseparable, like the four directions of a compass. So, you will hear these needs as the heart seeks to redirect you back into balance, and on the road to freedom. How cool is that? In this book, you'll be learning to listen to the subtle cues from the heart so you can tap in and lead the chariot.

The Four Faces of the Heart

In the traditional Buddhist literature, the four faces of the heart are called the *Brahmaviharas*. I personally love the sound of it. So, of course I translated them in a way that I find most applicable to us, modern sassy mega bosses.

1. Love: Love is simply our innate wish for ourselves and others to be happy. When you think about love and relationships, and when you tell yourself, friends, and lovers, "I love you," what you're really saying is "I support you to be happy." We have been conditioned to exist desperately in relation to love, from a place of lack and scarcity. This couldn't be further from the truth. You were born knowing how to love and be loved.

2. Self-compassion and compassion: Let's just take a moment to recognize that everyone, with no exception, just like you and me, wishes for the same two things: to be happy

and free of suffering. Compassion is action based—it happens through movement, the doing of something to alleviate your suffering and the suffering of others.

3. Joy: This is a state of unshakeable contentment and your innate ability to delight in the happiness, well-being, and success of yourself and others.

4. Wisdom: This, you could say, is the secret sauce. It is the ground from which the other qualities work sustainably. Traditionally translated as equanimity, wisdom is an inner-calmness, a state of inner-balance that supports you to see reality clearly, without the added filters of the untrained mind. It's the capacity to keep your heart open and in direct access to its innate qualities, in the face of your own suffering and the suffering of others.

On the spiritually sassy path, you will learn to connect with the heart on demand. As fast as you can go and get a quick fix, you will learn to turn to the supportive, inner, wise guidance. We will be training ourselves to become fluent in this internal modality. The beautiful part about this work is that once we are in touch with the spiritual heart, we impact everyone and everything around us. We are no longer a radio wave of stress. We are a radio wave of compassion and kindness and creativity and courage and inspiration.

In my teaching, the heart is where you have access to your inner, wise teacher. It's our doorway to the part of our self that doesn't experience suffering, even when we believe our whole self is experiencing suffering. In some teachings the heart will be the super-subtlemind, or the superconscious mind, or the soul, or the higher self. It's whatever you want to call it, whatever feels true to you. For me, calling it "the heart" is a way of bringing a common vocabulary and making it something we can all understand, so we can learn that it's through the path of the heart that we become free. Some people call it the spirit. They say, "Spirit told me this and that." I want you to shift away from looking outside for answers and look completely within. This entire book is about going inside.

COMING OUT OF THE SPIRITUAL CLOSET

First things first: let's come out and be proud. *Spiritually Sassy* is all about honoring your uniqueness, your authentic self. Spiritual teachers will tell you that we're all one. But when you walk into a space and you are visibly different from everyone in the room, and the world outside feels unsafe and unwelcoming to your "difference," oneness in a realistic sense can feel quite false. This has definitely been my experience. Usually what we mean when we say "different," even if we're saying it in a positive way, is "other." You can only be "other" when viewed through a mainstream (white, cis, heteronormative) lens. So even though oneness is a nice idea, and even though spiritually I agree with it in theory, the world we live in today isn't there yet. When you feel like you have to pry open crawl spaces before you can begin to feel any sense of safety or belonging—when that is your reality, the idea of being ONE feels false. So, I am calling bullshit on this notion. While it may be true (that is, if color blindness/racism/homophobia weren't a thing) that spiritually, if we stripped ourselves down to our hearts, we are in fact all one, I don't find the concept relevant. I am instead calling for a celebration of differentness, a celebration of your unique magic that you came here to share. Your magic will set you free.

Hopefully we will all eventually arrive at this empowered place, but until then it can be incredibly painful to hide parts of yourself or try to conform to mainstream standards, or simply feel the pain and shame of not fitting in, not feeling accepted, being discriminated against or shunned. This hurts me to write because as I type, I think back on my own experience of trying to find my voice personally, spiritually, and even sexually. I came out of the closet not only as queer but as a spiritual person, and me celebrating my individuality wasn't for everyone. I had to learn that that was okay. I am not for everyone. It was a risk worth taking, and the payoff has been profound. I found myself, I found my people, and I found my mission in life. Maybe when you come out of your metaphoric closets, you will not be for everyone. But I need you to trust that you will find the tribe, the purpose, the abundance, the healing, and you will do it by being true to you, the You with a capital Y.

~~Be Like Everyone Else~~ Be Yourself

I want you to shift the idea of what you've been told about being different. I am different because of what I have going on inside of me, which is different from what you have going on. And of course, we have external differences, too. When we start to clean up our mental obscurations and build a bridge to the heart, we realize that the fact that we're not all the same, that we're made up of a multitude of differences, is so beautiful. But first we have to do individual work, honor our own differences, our own beauty, and then we'll be able to see beauty in other people.

But it wasn't easy to come to this understanding. As a queer man of color I was sick and fucking tired of walking into spiritual spaces and having a straight white man teaching me things. I was done with that. I never felt at home. Even in Nepal, on a thirty-day silent retreat, there were 250 people there but only three people of color! There was one black woman, one black man, and me. This recognition of differentness has deeply informed my practice and my teaching, and this book is an invitation to bring spirituality to everybody, especially those of us who have never felt at home in a world that puts down our differences.

Only you know what your special sauce is. This is what makes living fun. This is what makes you beautiful. Let's stop lying to ourselves and believing we're the same and instead make our uniqueness part of our spiritual life. Your personality is actually an expression of your heart in this world. It is meant to help guide you on your unique path. You were born to laugh and play and dance in the way only you can. It is how you find your tribe, your mission. It is the color/pattern/texture/fragrance of your heart. Stop hiding it. Stop hiding! The world needs your signature scent, your pop of radiant color, your bold pattern. I need you. We need you. You need you.

When we talk about activating your innate superpowers, we are talking about inviting everybody you come into contact with to do the same. People will be inspired by the way you speak, the way you carry yourself, the way you walk, the way you hold your fork, the way you dress. We are told that when we are living our dreams and doing what we love, it's selfish and vain, but I am here to help you redesign this vocabulary and its whole narrative.

Maybe you're excited, maybe you're scared. That's okay. This is all about honoring where you are and doing it anyway. Everyone has an Achilles' heel. We've all got shit. And generally that shit comes out to say "Boo!" when you need it to be quiet the most—you know, those moments when you could use courage or self-compassion and instead you get an onslaught of self-doubt, or insecurity, or guilt, or fear, or anxiety, or depression, or self-pity, or self-flagellation, or what have you. Or maybe you're like me and your whole world has fallen apart, so you are seeking answers, seeking truth, seeking yourself. Wherever you are, your stuff will find you. You get the idea: the stuff shows up differently in everyone, and it's our job to bring it to the light and stop letting it run our lives. Let's get started. I guarantee you that you will see yourself to the other side of the bridge.

The Current Story of You

Step 1: Know your story to change your story.

To find out who you are, you need to first understand who you *think* you are. What are the belief systems that keep you stuck? We need to know this so we can tear them down and rebuild. The story of you is often not the true You. Earlier, I shared with you a little bit about my story and what led to my awakening. When my life started to break down, so did the story. There's often an impetus to our awakenings; how we arrive will look different for each of us. My story involved a definition of success that didn't match who I was. I had to look at that story from all angles and then figure out what was left. Think of it like stepping out of the movie into the seats of the audience and being witness to what's playing out. Consider: What creates your story loop? What are you ruminating on? What are you worrying about? How are you sabotaging your personal freedom and your ability to cultivate internal success and external abundance in your life? That's what we're going to look at in this chapter.

UNDERSTANDING THE MIND

Let's begin with the mind. You have to use the power of the mind to create a little space between You and the thoughts you're having. This is the first step in locating You. You are not who you think you are. *Uh . . . what is this guy talking about?* you may be thinking. *I'm a human being, that's who I am—I'm me!* Indeed you are, I cannot argue with that, but what I'm referring to when I say "You're not who you *think*" are literally the thoughts happening inside your head. "I'm smart," you may say, "my thoughts are intelligent and help me make decisions." And that would be true. You are brilliant, and many of your thoughts are helpful, but most of them are probably not. Experts estimate that the mind thinks between 60,000 and 80,000 thoughts a day. That's an average of 2,500 to 3,300 thoughts per hour.[1] Our work in this chapter is to understand the quality of those thoughts and ultimately redesign our relationship to them. Understanding the quality of our internal landscape will give us the information we need to set ourselves free. Acknowledging the role and power of thoughts is the first step.

Feelings influence thoughts, and vice versa. Together, they influence action. Now, we already acknowledged that many of our thoughts are useful and brilliant. But I want to talk about the thoughts we have that tend to be incredibly delusional. These thoughts are really not to be trusted. They are persuasive fuckers, thoughts—living in your mind, never shutting up, having you believe a constant flow of lies about who you are and how the world sees you. For example, how many times a day do you call yourself stupid? How about ugly? How many times a day do you try to convince yourself you'll never have love, that you're not worthy, that you should just give up on your goal? The more negative thoughts you entertain, the more you start to believe that they *are* You. No! They aren't.

You have spent your life listening to lies, and it's time to take back control and become the mega boss of your mind. This boss is wise, not aggressive or reactive. To be the mega boss of your mind, you must be a proactive bystander, watching the theater play out with a smirk on your face, your head shaking. You can be such a boss that you will be amused by it, "silly mind," and never, ever dragged down by it. You know better, wise boss. The thing about thoughts is that they think themselves. They are spontaneous, automatic, and they really don't need any help from you. Fighting them doesn't work because they are irrational and random. Getting into a thought fight with yourself is totally futile. "Shut up! Stop it, I hate myself, ugh!" You will be entering a nonstop negative thought/insult cycle . . . with yourself. Instead of talking to yourself, you will learn, with practice, to sit back and just watch—and be the boss.

So, rather than attempting to control thoughts, which would be futile, we must focus on what is within our control: our relationship to them. We must stop seeing each thought as requiring action or reaction. When we do this, they get so much quieter. Even the most negative and anxious ones begin to settle down because they no longer get a reaction from You. Negative thoughts love the negative thought/insult cycle! When this loving witnessing happens, you are uncovering your nature and reconnecting with the heart. When you stop engaging, like children, thoughts calm down and go back to drawing, or whatever, quietly. It's kind of like letting a child who's throwing a fit cry it out while you go about your business. You are training your mind to depend less on your reactions. Knowing a reaction isn't coming, eventually thoughts calm down and stop crying. We've got to make the conscious choice to let our mind throw a fit while we gracefully sit back and watch, letting the storm pass instead of getting caught up in it and emotionally thrashed around.

Quick Practice:
Observe Your Thoughts Like a Mega Boss

Note: Remember, a boss isn't judgmental. Just observe without judgment or labeling. Be silent in yourself and just watch.

- Be wherever you are. You can sit, stand, be commuting to work or relaxing on your couch, it doesn't matter.

- Set a timer for five minutes and simply observe your mind thinking without engaging.

- Observe any mental stories like anger, doubt, fear, or guilt. Just observe; don't get involved.

The problem is that we usually never make it that far, to the observing part. Instead, we're deep in it, involved, entangled, and invested. You have a craving, you satisfy it; you have the thought that you feel like crap, you eat a pint of ice cream; you have the thought that the person you like hasn't texted and therefore you feel bad about yourself and your image, so you take yourself shopping to feel better, spending money you don't have. Your current story probably includes regularly getting swept away by thoughts and feelings, which lead to behavior, which is driven by the desire to feel better. The intention is good—a part of your polarized mind is trying to protect you—but how often, when we follow the whims of our minds, do our choices and behaviors support our heart? We must learn to know better and to choose wiser.

The Fear/Reactivity Cycle (Circus)

Buddhist psychology says that feelings arise first; then the feelings get processed through the mind, thoughts claim the feelings, and then we react. This is what I like to call the reactivity circus. Why? Because it's a fucking circus. We are constantly believing the way we think and feel and then reacting to our thoughts and feelings as if they were the only reality. What if we knew that what we thought and felt about life had nothing to do with the way we wanted to live? What if it was just conditioning? Thoughts are passing through you, not originating from you. Just as thoughts think themselves without help from you, so do feelings. This is how it works: you have a pleasant feeling, which results in a positive thought, so you seek out something that will perpetuate that pleasant feeling.

This is the problem. We're constantly trying to hold on to and exaggerate the good things. We cling to these feelings, which leads us into all kinds of complications, but the truth is, we're always only navigating three main types. This is talked about in the Four Foundations of Mindfulness in Buddhist psychology, which explains that all feelings have one of three flavors: pleasant, unpleasant, or neutral.[2] We seek to hold on to pleasant states. When we have an unpleasant state, we feel aversion, and when we have a neutral state, we quickly try to find a way to get back to the pleasant state. When we're feeling good, we reach out for more pleasant experience: ice cream or a glass of wine or maybe gossip. While these things may make you feel good, they are not good for you.

A moment of liberation happens when you can take the perspective of a witness to your own experience—when you are able to be in such close contact with your heart that you can witness this reactivity circus playing out. A feeling enters, a thought comes, and the reaction/impulse is about to form, but *instead* of giving in, you *notice*, take a breath, listen to the heart, and then *choose*. You have a choice! We believe we have no choice because we're hooked on autopilot. Feel think react, feel think react, again and again. But when we start to connect to the heart, we can choose, and we have access to free will. When you notice and observe, that's the heart space you're in. That is heart training. It's that simple.

Think of all the ways the untrained mind tries to distract you and take you away from your heart like clouds covering the sun. The clouds are the thoughts, the seasons are the emotions, and behind all of that is the sun, always shining. So, no matter what you have going on, no matter your internal landscape, no matter the flavor of the internal chaos, you always have access to the heart (your sun)—this solar energy, blasting warm potential and light. We're not our thoughts; we're not our feelings, either; we are what's beneath them—the sun.

How you think is guided by the belief system that you have internalized about yourself and the world. But these beliefs are not necessarily who you are. This is so profound, but most of us don't have access to this subtle understanding. We haven't been trained to notice how, when there's a little unpleasant feeling arising, BOOM, we are immediately headed into catastrophizing, having completely left the present moment. The body begs you to return. Maybe you start to bite your nails. Biting your nails is one way the body communicates and begs you to start inhabiting it again, to come on back into the present moment. By now, we know: the belief systems we've internalized are a result of our default mind running unchecked. How empowering to know that with a little awareness, you can intervene and train your mind to operate with a new default. You are in charge.

Beliefs

Let's look at beliefs for a moment. I want you to think of the mind as a house. Here you are on your spiritual journey, starting to wake up to some of the habits of the mind. You wake up in this house and you have no fucking clue who built it, who furnished it, who chose the wallpaper, who decorated. You're sort of in awe, like, "What is all this stuff?" Imagine everything in that house was a representative of your belief systems. The big table that's in the dining room represents your relationship to food. The mirror in the bathroom—that's your relationship to your body. The windows and the curtains represent your self-worth and how much love you think you deserve.

The house is so full of this moldy, dusty furniture, it's so cluttered in there, that you have no access to your heart. All the clutter is blocking access to the blueprint to your freedom. You can't even move through the house without getting hooked on one negative belief after another—*This furniture and wallpaper are bad and they make me feel bad!* You have the potential to not only be in this house and witness it for what it is without becoming reactive, but you also have the potential to redesign it completely in a style that represents who You are.

First, we must acknowledge that the vast majority of the ways we feel, think, and react to life are pre-existing in our mind stream, and through the environments and people we were raised in and around they become dusty furniture representing the unskillful belief systems in our minds. They are unconscious, automatic, and so without awareness that over time, these belief systems, emotional reactions, and thought patterns have become your identity. But when you choose to wake up to the house you are currently living in and realize, *Oh my goodness, all this furniture does not fit the interior design of my heart—the way I relate to food, the way I relate to my body, the way I relate to romantic partners, the way I relate to fashion, art, music, you name it—it's all based on belief systems that aren't truly me,* that's when the heart redesigning can begin.

These beliefs fuel the narrative of your mind stream. Remember, you have choices. You can choose to find a quick fix the moment you become aware of some difficult thought or emotion, getting high by doing things to distract you from what you know or numb you from dealing with the challenging thoughts and feelings that are arising. Or, you can get free by staying in the house and choosing to dust the furniture, scrape off the mold, until eventually you get to the place where you bring the old furniture out into the backyard and set that shit on fire and maybe even get out the hammer and start breaking down the walls and build a whole new house with a whole new foundation. Little by little. The point is, you always have these two choices: get high or get free. Do what you've always done, or make a choice. Keep perpetuating the cycle of suffering, or choose You. The more you choose You, the more it will feel natural to do so. It will hurt less and be less overwhelming. Little by little.

On the spiritually sassy path and in this spiritually sassy mega boss curriculum, you are gifted the tools to rebuild your entire house and redesign it with belief systems that support your heart-led freedom.

Now, I want you to take a look around your house. I want you to honestly assess where you are in this moment in your life. With the following exercise, we'll look at your life holistically and see what is and is not in alignment. At the end of the day, all any of us wants is to be in alignment with as many areas of our life as possible. And what is the measure for alignment? The heart, of course. When we are in alignment with the heart, that is when we have sustainable happiness, that is when we're living from truth. The goal is to have all cylinders firing. And if not all, then *most* cylinders firing. You are on a mission to live your best life possible, a mission to improve what needs improving, giving attention to the parts of you that are begging for a little more love. This is the big idea. And it, too, stems from the heart. What radiates from your heart, the truth of who You are, should be free flowing into all areas of life, and if it's not, you will know where your personal work lies.

Part 1: How Am I Doing and What Do I Want?

Sometimes this talk of the heart and alignment doesn't seem tangible, so we will speak in wishes for now. Following each question, write about what's working well and what needs attention. Then, write your wish for yourself. Let this wish be ultimate, true, and sincere. Trust it, even if you have doubts about how it will happen. Write your answers below or in your journal.

1. **Self-love (Your Relationship to You)**

   What's working?

   What needs work?

   My wish

2. Relationships (Friendship/Community/ Romantic)

What's working?

What needs work?

My wish

3. Family

What's working?

What needs work?

My wish

4. Spiritual

What's working?

What needs work?

My wish

5. Work (Your Career, or Whatever Your Work Is in the World)

What's working?

What needs work?

My wish

Part 2: Are You Ready to Change?

You've identified which areas you want to give more attention to in your journey, and you've made a heart wish for how you'd like to change. Now the hard part: taking action, actually changing your behavior in service of living your best life. Change is hard, friends.

The following exercise is meant to prepare you for change and see what is blocking you from doing what you say you want to do. I mean, you're probably all too familiar with your excuses for why you haven't taken action or why you've attempted and then failed, but it's pretty amazing what a little fierce wisdom can do to break down the excuse narratives we tend to build our lives around.

There are five stages of change: 1) Precontemplation, 2) Contemplation, 3) Preparation, 4) Action, and 5) Maintenance. These stages are often used for overcoming addiction, but they can be applied to almost any area of your life that you want to change.[3]

As you respond to the following questions, reflect on part 1 of this exercise and hold in your mind the specific wishes you have for your life and what is required to make those wishes reality.[4]

On a scale of 1-10, how important is it for you to change?

1   2   3   4   5   6   7   8   9   10

On a scale of 1-10, how confident are you that you can succeed?

1   2   3   4   5   6   7   8   9   10

On a scale of 1-10, how ready are you to make a change?

1   2   3   4   5   6   7   8   9   10

What are the pros and cons of **not** changing?

What are the pros and cons of changing?

Why do you want to make this/these changes in your life? Dig deep.

What is preventing you from changing?

What things, people, or behaviors have helped you change in the past?

What will help you right now?

What barriers can you see ahead, and how can you eliminate them?

What has **not** helped in the past and what can you replace those things with?

Who can you turn to for support?

List 3–5 actions you can take, starting now, to progress toward your wishes. Start small.

1.

2.

3.

4.

5.

YOU CAN TEACH AN OLD DOG NEW TRICKS

So now you know what's in the way, what actions you intend to take, and what your deep heart needs are. Yet the pesky mind is still in the way. The mind, in this case, is the old dog. It is the hardest thing to change and get on board with what the rest of you wants. But I have good news: neuroplasticity. It's a beautiful thing that science has discovered. Research actually proves that the brain is in fact plastic, meaning it's flexible as opposed to fixed.[5] Our brains may be hardwired for certain instincts, like survival and negativity bias (more about this later), but for everyday beliefs and habits (the ones that keep you stuck), you have the power to train the brain to learn new habits.[6] Little by little, the brain responds to change and can, with practice, transform behaviors driven by old thought patterns. When you introduce a new response (such as a pause or choice that interrupts automatic thoughts, feelings, and behaviors), the brain can rewire itself to start to expect this new response. I'm not a neuroscientist by any stretch of the imagination, but the basics of human evolution and how the brain works are pretty fascinating, and I want to share them with you.

Wired for Survival

Being wired for survival in our modern world unfortunately means we are naturally wired for anxiety, fear, and negativity. I have immense gratitude for my brain, my limbic system, and nervous system. It has kept me alive all these years. It alerts me to dangers and threats. But the not-so-useful part of this wiring is that . . . well, we're not in danger all that often anymore. So the brain, only trying to help us out, throws us into panic/anxiety/fear/negativity mode over pretty much everything: a text, a presentation, a call, an email, a rejection, a bad day, you name it. You have to remember, though, that this is just the brain doing what it does. It is our job as wise hearts to know better and discern the difference between a real threat and a bad day or an awkward moment.

The amygdala is responsible for regulating our emotions and all of our emotion-fueled behavior. Interestingly, this means it is involved in our behavior related to sex, food, and drugs. But the area where the most research on the amygdala has been done is its integral role in the way we experience fear. Studies show that the amygdala is activated in response to stimuli like fearful faces, fear-inducing images, and fear cues.[7] Think of this activation as an alert to you: it's your brain sending you a signal to be afraid, stressed, freaked out.

Our ancestors needed this threat- and danger-detecting default mindset because we didn't have access to iPhones, gated communities, or Seamless. We had to run out into the field, into the jungle, into the forest to hunt our food and build shelter. There was so much danger out there, and this neural alarm system was a huge reason for our survival. Not so much anymore, though. The world has really changed, but that old part of the brain has not adapted. So, it is our job as wise hearts to rise above this archaic mechanism and know the difference between real danger and mere discomfort, creating mental space between what's real and what's the brain doing its old fear thing. We all have the potential to redesign what we'll call our *default mindset* to a more functional one for today that is compassionate and wise. Imagine yourself reacting differently next time freak-out o'clock rolls around. Instead of getting into an anxious spiral and losing it, you can relax, knowing your mind is just doing its thing. This is observing your mind like a science-based boss.

Wired for Change

The beautiful thing about science is that it affirms what we already know and what the great spiritual traditions have been teaching for thousands of years. Mindfulness, the ancient practice of focusing awareness on yourself and your experience, goes hand in hand with neuroscience. When we observe our mental patterns, we teach the brain new responses—we rewire the brain. The study of neuroplasticity says that the brain is adaptable; brain structure can change as we introduce new experiences, as we learn, and as we adapt to the changing world around us.

Every repeated thought or emotion we have reinforces a neural pathway. What power that is, my friends! I need a moment. Every thought and every emotion we have essentially tells the brain: do more of this, feel more of this, think more of this. It sets a pattern of being for the brain.

As you can imagine, change is hard but possible. Every day, with every thought, you have an opportunity to teach your brain a new way of being. Will you choose to teach more stuckness, or will you choose to teach freedom?

Think of developing neuroplasticity like working out. You go to the gym and work out so you can be fit and toned; otherwise, your muscles atrophy. Same with the mind. Meditation, mental pauses, mantras, affirmations, observing the mind—these practices work out the mind and retrain it to support the real You. Otherwise it's on automatic, not necessarily trying to hurt you, but untrained and sometimes running haywire. The mind wants and needs you to train it just as your body wants you to move it and keep it healthy. Just as your mind is wired to protect you, so too is your mind wired for change. It wants to help you! It just needs you to show it how. It is important for us to know that the mind goes far beyond the physical workings of the brain. The brain and the mind are not the same thing, but they do work interdependently with one another. And as you change your mind, you change the architecture of your brain.

So how do we change? With small, consistent actions. Every moment is an opportunity to harness neuroplasticity.

You absolutely *can* feel, think, and behave differently, and your mind will support you. But okay, the brain, the heart, the mind, the chatter, the real me . . . blah blah blah. What do I *do*?

The big (and so simple) wisdom in all of this is that the breath leads us out of our heads and back into our body. When we come back to our body (consistently, every moment, again and again, tirelessly), we return to the heart, and in doing so we teach the brain a new habit. When we train the mind to observe the mind instead of becoming entangled with it, we train ourselves to lean back into a truer reality, beyond the chaos and fear. Think of "back" as where the heart is, where the breath is, and entangled reality as the day-to-day stress, creeping anxiety, chaos, and chatter of the mind. The truer reality is always inside you, but you have to lean back to access it. The way we access it is through breathwork and meditation, through mantras and affirmations. We then teach ourselves to lean back to that truer place within us, more and more often, until it feels like home. Eventually, returning to this place becomes the new default. We lead our attention away from the conditioned mind and back into the heart space.

THE INNER CRITIC/HOW THE MIND HOLDS YOU BACK

I was doing a talk for my first book tour. In the audience were some very serious meditators. When it was time to share a story about my life, I said, "I want to tell you about Bianka with a K." I went on, "Bianka is fabulous. She's loud, funny . . . and vicious." And everyone started laughing because they knew who Bianka was. Bianka is my inner critic. Bianka is narrating, judging, and being critical of everything I experience; she's labeling and writing people off before they've had the opportunity to surprise me, before I even get a chance to connect with their goodness.

She's quick to jump to negative and paranoid conclusions about almost everything . . . if I let her. Why do I call it Bianka, why do I give my inner critic a name? Because giving it a name creates space between it and the true me and helps me know the difference. There's Me and there's Bianka. Knowing the difference empowers Me.

Bianka's story is millions of years old. The inner critic is an aspect of the fear response that has no place in our modern environment, where we (most of us) don't have to protect ourselves anymore from serious physical threats, like a lion in the wild, hunt our food, and keep our families safe. With very few threats to protect you from, this aspect of the human mind is a bit displaced, and so it runs wild in your everyday, modern life, inventing threats, fears, and anxieties out of regular, everyday life. To your poor mind, you feeling nervous about a presentation is as dangerous as a lion chasing you. You having a panic attack about whether or not you can start dating again is also a lion. You being afraid to ask for a raise: another lion. You not trying something new out of fear: a lion. How many things in your life is your brain turning into a lion? Our inner critic is the fear response gone wild. But guess what? There's no lion! We can all relax. Hah! As if it were that easy. We have to outsmart our own minds, and learning to label thoughts, even name them, is one way to do that.

In the last chapter you practiced observing thoughts non-judgmentally; now I want you to try doing this for a week with a focus on how you talk to yourself. The most important relationship is the one you have with yourself. You've heard this before, I'm sure, but just think about it. Your truest home is in your body; the most intimate and vulnerable conversations are the ones you've had with yourself. It's not often we stop to pay attention to the way we speak to ourselves when no one can hear.

Self-Talk Diary[8]

Using the space on the next page, or on your phone or in a journal, notice and record the quality of your thoughts for the next week. Keep a tally of as many thoughts as you can. Start to become aware of how you are talking to yourself. In order to change the pattern, you have to know what to look for.

At the end of the week, see how you did. Bringing attention to the quality of your thoughts will help you to stop identifying with and believing them, and help you build your awareness muscle.

	Monday	Tuesday	Wednesday	Thursday	Friday	Saturday	Sunday
Neutral							
Kind/ Supportive							
Unkind							
Positive/ Affirming							
Straight up mean							
Not even my worst enemy would say that to me							

Labeling Thoughts

We each have default ways of thinking that become our patterns. Typically, our thoughts fall into one of the following pattern types. As you read through these, look back at your thought log and notice how you tend to talk to yourself and, more broadly, how you think. Check off any that are familiar to you.

Filtering

Do you have a special ability to overlook all the positive things and have laser focus on the one negative thing going on?

Black and White Thinking

This is all-or-nothing thinking, with no room for complexity or nuance, as in, "If I don't do it perfectly, I'm a failure."

Overgeneralization

"I did ____ once and it was terrible, therefore all ____ are terrible and I'll never do _____ again."

Jumping to Conclusions

"I've never done it, but if it's anything like _____, it'll be terrible, too." "I don't know them but they'll probably suck."

Catastrophizing

It's merely raining, but to you there's a stage-five hurricane and you're in the middle of it. If anything goes wrong or not as planned, your life pretty much falls apart.

Personalization

It's all about me! I can never mess up because everyone's well-being depends on my being perfect. If I mess up, everything and everyone will be impacted.

Control Fallacies

It's all my fault. Whatever is going wrong, I probably caused it.

Blaming

I feel too vulnerable to be accountable for my behavior, so instead I blame others for what's wrong or what has happened. It's everyone else's fault.

Shoulds

There is a way I believe people should behave, and if they don't behave that way, then I will become emotionally triggered. If I break my own rules of behavior, I will likely lash myself with guilt and regret for it.

Emotional Reasoning

I feel sad; therefore I am a depressed person. I feel ugly; therefore I am ugly. I let my feelings guide me. Whatever they say, I believe.

There's a lot going on inside of us. Understanding how the mind works can be incredibly empowering so that we don't feel like we're being swept away by every thought and emotion. Instead, we can recognize our own patterns and stop ourselves in our tracks—caught ya! The mind is always going, doing what it does, so awareness is a full-time job. If you start to catch yourself in one of these thought patterns, lean back into your wisdom.

The wisdom of your heart is your greatest antidote, and the beautiful thing is that it's always there for you.

Replacing Limiting Beliefs

Obviously, the untrained, neurotic, conditioned mind plays tricks on us. What the mind says and narrates is not an accurate representation of reality. But the tricky thing about thoughts is that they've been with us our whole lives. As a result, we probably have some deep-seated and untrue beliefs about ourselves that are in dissonance with our hearts. They need to not only be called out, but replaced.

Write down ten limiting beliefs that hold you back. Next to each one, write a replacement belief, something that opposes it and asserts a truer version of you.

Here's my list of beliefs that feed Bianka. It's vulnerable to share this, but vulnerability is power, so here goes:

Limiting Belief	Replacement Belief
1. I have to struggle.	I can live with ease.
2. I can't ever be 100%.	I am always whole.
3. I don't belong.	Wherever I am, I belong.
4. No one can love me.	I am lovable!
5. I'm sick.	I am healthy.
6. I can't ever have abundance.	I am abundant and I have what I need.
7. My body is gross.	My body is beautiful, strong, and sexy.
8. I'm a bad person.	I am innately good.
9. I'm a fraud.	I am qualified and confident.
10. I have nothing to offer.	I have experience and wisdom to offer; I am enough.

Write your lists below:

Limiting Belief	Replacement Belief
1. _____	_____
2. _____	_____
3. _____	_____
4. _____	_____
5. _____	_____
6. _____	_____
7. _____	_____
8. _____	_____
9. _____	_____
10. _____	_____

Look at what you wrote on the right side. Consider this your new manifesto. This is the first step in listening to your heart. Once you have the strength and awareness to clear away some of the mental trash, you can start to see clearly the truth of who you are. Stick it on your mirror, on your computer, or make it your screensaver. Do what you have to do to implant these new beliefs into your mind and let them be your guide from now on.

I like to return to the house metaphor. Imagine these ten limiting self-beliefs were pieces of furniture in your house. I'm asking you, the reader, to set this shit on fire in the backyard. And rather than going to Ikea, build ten new belief systems that are rooted in the ways you want to feel and think and act in the world. This is the magic trifecta that is going to support your high vision in the world. Each time we believe one of these limiting beliefs, we are inflaming the amygdala, reinforcing the belief, and sending a message to the whole body: believe this, act this way. We've got to tell a different story.

Using the Nervous System to Support New Ways of Being

The brain doesn't work alone, of course; it is in constant communication with our nervous system. The nervous system has two main parts: the sympathetic and the parasympathetic. We can think of the sympathetic nervous system as the way we react and respond to stress; it mobilizes the body's energy and resources during times of stress, while the parasympathetic nervous system conserves energy and resources during relaxed states, like in meditation, rhythmic breathing, and sleep. Stress—as in the flight/fight/freeze response—is thought to counteract the parasympathetic system, which works to promote maintenance feelings associated with rest, digestion, and relaxation.[9]

From its name, you may think the sympathetic part of the nervous system is the part that's resting and relaxing, but it's actually the part that sets us off into fight, flight, or freeze mode. Just as the amygdala helps us respond to threats, the sympathetic nervous system enables us to respond to stress. This mechanism is very primal and asks us to react immediately when the alarm goes off, often with a fight/flight/freeze response.

Through the parasympathetic system we have access to the wise heart, to a sense of rest, nurturing, and well-being. In this mode, we get to respond to life rather than react. The best way to access the parasympathetic function of the nervous system is by implementing a daily practice of relearning how to take deep belly breaths. An ordinary anxious person anywhere in the world is breathing up to sixteen times per minute, so very short, shallow breaths. We're talking about creating a breathing pattern (four to six times per minute) that supports a healthy conversation between the brain, the nervous system, the gut, and the heart. Doing this breathwork, simply slowing it down, teaches the sympathetic system to chill out and the parasympathetic system to kick in more of the time. This breath practice strengthens the vagus nerve, which scientists call the "love nerve" in humans.[10] You see, simply by breathing, we can support a new message and broadcast it all over the body: relax, relax, relax. It's all connected, and in fact, I'll teach you a breathing practice later in this chapter that does just this (page 66).

CULTIVATING A LOVE BIAS

There's yet another thing we must watch out for, and it is called negativity bias. This is the thought pattern that only sees bad stuff (what a downer!). The Debbie Downer inside of you is incredibly powerful and can color so much of your experience. Negativity bias is the reason it hurts so much when we get rejected, when we fail, when we're told we're bad or not enough—it goes straight into the worst-case scenario. Much research has been done to understand this. In a study by John Cacioppo, a neuroscientist at the University of Chicago, participants were shown pictures that evoked positive feelings, pictures that evoked negative feelings, and pictures that evoked neutral feelings. He found that the negative stimuli created more electrical activity, showing that our brains, and therefore we, are more influenced by negative news than anything else.[11]

Just as the brain looks for threats in order to keep you safe, it is wired to look for negativity. Here, too, it is trying to protect you by sounding an alarm each time you're emotionally hurt. And this makes sense. Imagine what would happen if we didn't get an alarm when we were physically in danger. None of us would get very far in life. The body's response to trauma and emotional pain is so interesting because just like with physical pain, our bodies remember emotional pain.[12] The ways we have been conditioned to relate to pain and suffering have a way of sticking around for a long time. The brain, again, trying to help. We unintentionally replay, relive, self-sabotage, avoid, and repeat old patterns, developing all these behaviors to try to avoid future pain. We are all living in a constant interplay of trying not to get hurt. Your heart knows the difference between a real threat to your life and a perceived threat to your happiness and well-being—an actual lion or somebody from a dating app rejecting you—but your brain is still operating with archaic hardware.

What if we could build and flex our love and compassion reserves instead? Also, um, hello heart? Where are you? Where have you been while all this shit's been going down in my brain and nervous system? We've got threats and lions and alarms going nonstop. It's chaos. Where are you, heart? The heart has been there, honey, waiting for you to open the curtains and tap in. Lean back, it's there.

What if we could create an internal landscape that was less chaotic, more filled with thoughts like "I love you," "You are doing your best," and "I believe in you"? How different would it feel if that was your new default? Guess what? It's possible. You can absolutely turn the dial down on your perception of chaos and turn up the volume on love.

Thoughts, both positive and negative, are beyond powerful. And you probably have a number of positive thoughts every day. The positive ones are probably in constant conflict with the negative ones. Like, "Hey, shut up," or "I look nice today," or "I did well today, today was a good day," or "Good job." We actually have the power to cultivate positive thoughts and live a more positive reality as a result. We can do this in a number of ways.

Tuning into a frequency of love takes practice. Our new default has to be to NOTICE when we've left the present moment and gone into story, gone into limiting belief, drifted far away into future tripping and worrying or digging up the past.

In each moment, we are offered a choice: heart or story, heart or bullshit belief, heart or worry about things that haven't happened yet. Practice means choosing the heart more often. Let it become your default. Notice when you've left the present moment. Usually when we've left the present moment, we start to add stories to everything we're experiencing. We get far away from reality, lost in fiction. The breath becomes shallow and we enter fight/flight/freeze mode; our way of seeing life becomes reactive rather than skillfully responsive. One of the most powerful things you can do is to breathe. Rather than your breath becoming short and shallow, the breath becomes long and deep. Breath alone can help redesign your reactivity response. Breath is one of the greatest healing tools.

What Love Sounds Like

The wise heart speaks in "hits" or "downloads," as we'll call them. But it is said that the only way to hear or receive these messages is in the gaps, the in-between moments when we're tapped into something other than internal chatter and chaos. You see how this all connects? More mental space, more choice in each moment, leads to more quiet for the heart to come in and be heard.

When the heart speaks, you may receive it as spontaneous knowing. I say *knowing* because it is nonverbal; it just *is*. We can try our best to describe it with words, but there is no vocabulary for it. When it happens, it will be a very individual, beautiful experience of creating a deep bond with your heart. Though we may not have language for it, we have this understanding already. Think of a time when you've had intuition, when you've "just known" something, when you've said, "I don't know, I just know it in my heart." Those kinds of things are how the heart speaks.

We are in constant contact with the heart, even if we hear it for only a moment when we meditate or create space in the chattering, chaotic mind stream some other way. For most people, the heart download goes unnoticed, which is why the inner chatter goes right back on full power once the moment passes. With this work, the spiritually sassy curriculum, you can disentangle and tap in more of the time.

The Role of the Body

All this talk about the mind and heart, but the body, too, is essential to this work. Like I said, honey, it is all connected. The body is how you tap in, the gateway and the pathway. It is your primal vessel; it's where you have access to the heart. The reason we work to understand the mind is so we can spend less time trapped in there. We no longer need to let our mental experience dominate our entire experience. You have a body, now get in it! Really be inside yourself. During one of the first teachings I received, one of my teachers in the North Himalayas said to me, "Sah, come back to your body." At the time I was such a beginner, I didn't know anything about the mind-body-heart connection. Everything was so literal to me. I was like, "What the fuck do you mean, 'come back to my body?' I *am* in my body." But a little later I realized what he meant. When we fully inhabit the body, we are in the present moment, and when we are in the present, we can hear the heart. This mind work is all so we can move our attention down, out of the head, out of stories about the past and future, into the body and eventually into the heart. The hope is that we reside there. That is the work. It's what I believe we've come here to learn.

Reconnecting with the heart is having access to choice. We need to go inside to figure out why we are acting the way we're acting, why we are in this perpetual spiral of blaming and pointing fingers instead of looking inward when we feel triggered. Looking inside when you feel disconnected will set you free. It's inside of you where you'll find the blueprint for your personal freedom.

Below is a meditation meant to help you stop discursive thinking and enter the gaps where you have access to your heart and a language beyond thoughts. Use it anytime you need help remembering you're not your thoughts.

Gibberish Meditation Adapted by Osho

This mediation offers a vocal release. For three to five minutes (or longer), you are just going at it, and it sounds . . . well, like gibberish. I want you to lose yourself and make sounds you don't usually make. Use your voice to make sounds that don't make any sense. What this does is create a break in the stream of thoughts and feelings. When you're done, you'll have created an internal silence that allows space for the heart.

- Set a timer for five minutes and begin.

- Notice how you feel when you're finished.

- Notice the quality of your thoughts.

Hopefully, you feel reset in some way. Do this anytime for a quick mind cleanse.

The Power of Pause

Responding differently is a key tool on the path to freedom. Your body and your breath are your anchors in the present moment and the most powerful tools available. If you can learn to practice grounding yourself in your body, you can hear what the moment holds and choose. Every moment offers a choice: fear or love. One reaction is automatic, and one is considered. Love requires a pause. Fear is what happens automatically, without intention; it is what guides unskillful thoughts and reactions to life. Fear is what guides the story of you that doesn't match up to your potential, who you know you are inside. It's easy to choose love when we're not stressed or being triggered. But it's in the moments when we *are* challenged, when someone or something gets close to one of our sensitive spots and fear automatically makes us recoil, hide, get angry, feel insecure or worthless, or forget we are worthy of love and life—that's when we need the power of pause. But pause takes practice.

The single most important thing we can do to redesign the automatic, negative inner critic? It is what gives you life, what you were born doing. Relearn. How. To. Breathe. Before anything else, we have to have a breathing practice. Next is self-talk. Once we introduce the mantras, they become the default. As you're going about your day—brushing your teeth, fixing your hair in the mirror, sitting on the subway, driving to work, walking anywhere—try inserting random kind thoughts into your mind. This is the easiest, most tender little gift you can give yourself. Tell yourself you love you, that you are okay, that you are enough. Repeat one of the new beliefs you wrote down. Whichever one you need today, repeat it to yourself and let it be your mantra. And breathe. What a treat everyday life can be if you allow it.

The Humming Breath practice is a great way to calm down and create space between you and whatever is going on.

Humming Breath

This practice is a really powerful way to calm the nervous system, disentangle from the internal chatter, and create space. If there is no pause, we have to teach ourselves to pause.

- Keep your eyes closed.

- For a few moments, notice the sensations in the body and your internal landscape.

- Place your index fingers on the cartilage of your ears between the cheek and the ear.

- Take a deep breath, and as you breath out, gently press the cartilage, plugging your ears. You can keep the cartilage pressed.

- You're making a loud humming sound like a bee as you breathe out (mmmmmm).

- Take very deep breaths, as much air as you can, and exhale as long as you possibly can.

- Practice for ten breaths.

No matter how far we think we are on the spiritual path and living in our power, the Bianka, the inner critic, still creeps in. The more creative it becomes, the more creative we must become. We simply continue to uplevel, honey. If you think your suffering ends with one breathing exercise, with one aha moment, think again. This work is continuous. We must always be working toward heart alignment. If you were perfectly aligned already, you wouldn't be here on Earth with the rest of us, working our shit out. The least we can do is try not to work our shit out on each other.

The goal is to replant the garden of your mind with so many supportive seeds, do so many virtuous deeds, be so deeply aligned in intention, speech, and action, that it relaxes the mind to be in complete connection with the heart. This is the path. But don't judge yourself or get hooked and upset if you've done all this work and tended your karmic garden and all of a sudden, that creepy little voice is like, "Hi bitch, I'm back," and you dwell on it, beat yourself up, and get hooked back in. When you arrive at the moment when you're finally not taken by every internal or external stimulus, you'll know you have done your work. Little by little. You notice it, maybe you dance a little dance with it, but then you come back—back into the heart, back into the present moment.

GETTING READY

Are you ready to have a new relationship with your self, with your future?

Imagine that there is space between the delusion of the negative/stressful/anxious thoughts and your clearer, more harmonious reality. Imagine your heart as the sun shining no matter what the weather. Imagine always having a deep knowing that the sun was always there, shining. Developing this knowing starts with awareness—awareness that there is a YOU above the you. Developing this knowing requires practice, a habitual method of reminding yourself that you are the sun. Say it now: I am the sun. I AM THE MOTHERFUCKIN' SUN! Soon you'll believe it.

In later chapters, you will learn practices to make this your reality, but first there is something you need to do: forgive. Forgive yourself and forgive others. This is the ultimate spiritual clearing for making room for the freedom that's arising in you.

You have investigated your stories and beliefs, your mind, body, and heart. Now it's time to take it one step further. To be fully accountable and responsible for our lives, for our actions, we must learn forgiveness and experience self-resolution. As we move into forgiveness, we will start to weed our internal garden, loosening up and removing these old stories and beliefs at their very roots.

4

Forgiveness
Boot Camp

Step 2: Learn to forgive yourself and those motherfuckers who have hurt you.

You want to measure your growth, your spiritual maturity? See if you can forgive people, including yourself. This is the ultimate test. This chapter will walk you through the meaning of forgiveness and give you tools to bring forgiveness into every day. Let's not waste any time. This very first exercise asks that you enter in on the other side of the forgiveness mirror— asking for forgiveness from those you have hurt.

THE POWER OF FORGIVENESS

There are gentle yet powerful actions you can take on your own, without involving anyone else or doing a deep dive into traumatic memories, that will help to shift the root of resentment. Forgiveness work can do this. So, let's begin.

Ask for Forgiveness
from Those You Have Hurt

Before we go any further with this concept, I want to ask that you take a few moments right now to ask for forgiveness from those you have hurt. Feel free to write it down or say it aloud. I challenge you, even if it feels awkward and vulnerable, to follow this through. Take your time. Use the breath as your anchor. Think of anyone in your recent or distant memory who has been hurt by you and ask to be forgiven now. This is not about blame, not about right or wrong—it's about clearing the heart. Take a deep breath. Notice how your heart feels when you've finished.

Use the powerful prompt:

"Hi, (person's first name), please forgive me, for all the ways that I have caused you harm intentionally or unintentionally with my thoughts, words, or actions."

Holding on to the past can be so painful. Wounds—old resentments, regret, past mistakes, guilt—make up the most insidious type of pain. This type of pain tends to hold on in hidden places and creep out when we least expect it, especially at times when what we really need is courage and kindness. This lack of forgiveness rears its ugly head in so many ways (anger, anxiety, low self-esteem, stress, depression) and creates a constant low-grade suffering where it's hard to pinpoint the source. We often mistake this painful state of being with our true self. It's not. It's just that it's covering your heart so that you can't hear your heart screaming from inside your chest, "I'm in here, don't forget about me! I'm right here!"

Think of forgiveness as your spiritual hot sauce—you can and should use it for everything. You know how Beyoncé made it cool to carry hot sauce in your purse?

Forgiveness is going to be what you carry around in your spiritual fanny pack and sprinkle on everything to bring out the innate peace, calm, and compassion that resides deep inside you—it is your essence.

In the last chapter you discovered your stories—what they're saying, how they've been in the driver's seat, and how they're holding you back. In this chapter, we're going to go a bit deeper, get under the hood a little, and look closely at where you need the power of forgiveness and compassion most in order to move forward and rewrite a new story of you.

What Is Forgiveness?

Forgiveness is radical acceptance. It's an innate quality, a superpower we all have. Forgiveness is the choice to be solution-based, to live longer, wiser, and kinder. We all have this potential. Each and every one of us has access to it and to the compassion that comes with it. In fact, forgiveness and compassion go hand in hand. Compassion is the wish, the intention, behind forgiveness—for yourself and others to be free of suffering.

Forgiveness is one of those words that sound silly or childish to the Western ear. Or, to the skeptic's ear, it may sound like spiritual bullshit. Were you ever taught about forgiveness—not just what the word means, but what it really involves? I wasn't. It's not a quality that's valued in our society. I was taught to suck it up, tuck it away, look strong (even if I wasn't), and . . . to be *right*. Acknowledging wrongdoing is associated with weakness and brings on feelings of shame that lie dormant in the mind and then go BOO! when it's time to do things that require our vulnerability, like loving, growing, and healing. So, you can see, forgiveness and compassion are essential as we start to rebuild and heal.

What forgiveness is not:

- Weakness
- Being a pushover
- Letting yourself or someone else off the hook

What forgiveness does:

- Dissolves anger, resentments, guilt, and shame
- Reduces stress, anxiety, and depression
- Increases well-being and helps you to live longer
- Rebuilds self-esteem
- Replenishes your internal resources of compassion and love
- Opens the heart

That last one though. I'm just going to let you sit with that for a hot minute. Imagine a world full of open hearts. Can you imagine it?

When I try to come up with examples of what a lack of forgiveness looks like in the real world, I think of parents and grandparents. Maybe you're lucky enough to have super-evolved relatives, but if you're like most of us, you can see the embodiment of their painful memories and stories haunting them in real time. Maybe they haven't been able to forgive their partner, their government, their parents. Maybe they took those resentments out on you, so the cycle has continued. Think for a moment about someone in your life who embodies lack of forgiveness for you. Now think about your own life. Maybe you're not so different. Perhaps your stories are younger, but they will grow older. It's time to nip them in the bud.

Think about your biggest pain right now, you know, the one that keeps you up at night or the one that, when triggered, plays nonstop in your mind. That's the one. Now think of yourself in twenty, thirty years still getting activated by that same story. Imagine how this might hold you back. Imagine what the pain might cause you to do once it's had all those years to brew and grow strong. All of the bits of story eventually become solid rock. You can think of this solid rock living in front of your heart and actually blocking you from knowing yourself. You believe this solid rock is who you are. It's not you. My love, you are part of the revolution of the heart. It's your time to heal. You have taken the courageous stand.

Take a moment to think about your own experiences of forgiveness. Even if this seems like an abstract exercise, challenge yourself. Start to think about who has hurt you. Think about how you've hurt yourself. If nothing comes to mind, remember that there are many subtle ways not forgiving plays out. Be willing to go through this process slowly. You can even repeat the affirmation "I am willing to forgive" to open yourself up to the process.

As you become ready to welcome the most transformed version of YOU, use this healing prompt for those who have caused you harm: "Hi (person's first name), I'm willing to forgive you for all the ways that you have caused me harm intentionally or unintentionally with your thoughts, words, or actions." And toward yourself: "I forgive myself for all the ways that I have caused myself harm intentionally or unintentionally with my thoughts, words, or actions."

Reflection

On a piece of paper or in your journal, write about all the ways your own lack of forgiveness has affected your life.

I sought forgiveness desperately when painful memories were blocking me in every direction, and the opening it created had a profound impact on my life. I know how debilitating certain narratives can be. Forgiveness is the path out and through. It is the direct path to the heart and to the present moment. Without forgiveness, you are blocked from the present moment. Literally. The key characteristics of anxiety and depression, for example, have roots in thoughts that are stuck in either the future or the past.[1] Being present sounds nice, but if you're suffering with these kinds of thoughts and energies, you are not available to the present moment; you will always be somewhere else. The cost of not making peace with the past and continuing on the path of resentment, worry, and fear is remaining blocked from peace and the present moment, where joy and healing happen.

FORGIVENESS AND TRAUMA

The effects of trauma are something we all experience, and the antidote to trauma is forgiveness. I know it sounds so simple, but the truth of it is, when we learn to forgive those who have hurt us and those we have hurt, and we learn to forgive ourselves for how we've treated ourselves while in states of confusion, we are able to establish a deeper connection with our hearts and recognize our essence. We're biologically wired to seek close and ongoing connections, so how can we follow through with this basic need of the heart if we are completely hooked on the traumatic memories playing on a loop in our mind?

Creating from Trauma

Creativity is hugely helpful in resolving trauma. This doesn't mean you become an artist. It just means you make an intentional effort to move the trauma and allow it to transform. Writing, painting, pottery, gardening, dancing—these kinds of activities support you to resolve with yourself whatever happened. Creativity can be a powerful, spiritual act, allowing us to make something new and healing out of old traumas. Making art is one way to bring the background—the events of the past and their pain—into the foreground in a safe way. When we open creative space, we allow for this. We need to find a creative outlet for trauma. We must create a ritual, which is an action with an intention—for me it's uninhibited dance—where we are diffusing the hold traumatic memory has on us.

You may have stored trauma in your body and not be aware of it because we do such a good job of becoming actors: "Nothing's wrong, I'm okay." A better and more honest mantra is, "Things are shitty, but I'm still okay," instead of lying to yourself and those around you. Lying and hiding your true experience perpetuates confusion. When we do this, we're giving more power to the traumatic memory and confusion and disempowering ourselves.

I'm not saying it's easy. Trauma is one of those nebulous things that we tuck deep inside of us but is ever present. It dictates so much of our lives, which is why it's so important to move it. Get it out, make something out of it for your own survival. Each time we're triggered or a memory spontaneously arises, we paint it with more shades of shame and guilt, as if the event and the memory weren't enough. This is not a life. No matter how much you have fucked up, or no matter how much other people have fucked up, we need to come to peace with whatever happened in the past. This is where forgiveness comes in. It's time to become the victor of the story and stop being the victim.

Bringing the Unconscious to the Light

Traumatic experiences do not get recorded in the brain the same way ordinary experiences do. They have not been thought through, reflected on, or placed into a context the way normal memories and experiences have. Instead, we repress them as soon as they happen, trying hard to forget them, and as a result, they affect our lives in ubiquitous and mysterious ways. What's bothering you may be impossible to talk about because it's happening completely on the unconscious level. Yet whatever it is will find its way into your life.

Once the story comes to the light, into conscious awareness, you have the power to reframe it. You can choose to see what happened from a new perspective with a new, compassionate understanding. Only then will it stop running your life.

Our limbic system is gathering information coming in through our senses—sight, sound, touch, smell, and taste. It's the prefrontal cortex that converts and translates this data into language and pictures and attaches meaning to them. When you're in a traumatic experience, this part of the brain actually shuts off, so all that's left to decipher what's going on are your senses.[2] The unprocessed sight, smell, sound, taste, and touch sensations get stored in the body somewhere without language or context. Part of what makes the work of forgiveness so powerful in relation to trauma is that you are opening up the floodgates of unprocessed sensations, allowing them to come up and out from the background of your mind and body to the foreground—to move, to be given new meaning, to be transformed (for example, by making and creating something from them). In these creative ways, we allow our bodies to speak. We MUST let our bodies speak. The forgiveness process is one part of healing at the core level. Movement and creativity are ways to allow your body to speak what's been unprocessed.

Unprocessed Trauma Unleashed

One way we might realize we have unprocessed trauma stored in our body is the smallest thing happens and we just rage out. Trust me honey, I know rage really well. This was my default. I didn't realize all the ways my parents didn't hold space for me to explore my queerness and how traumatic that was for me—being bullied and told in the locker room "you're a fag," then coming home to my parents and not being able to talk about what was happening to me. I had to process this on my own without any tools. So, growing up, I coped with my traumatic experience by becoming a rage machine.

The smallest little things would set me off, and this rage cycle kept me super stuck. Why? Because each time I raged out, I nurtured that rage seed so it would continue to blossom. I had a rage machine inside me; for others, it might be shutting down and going into silent mode. Other people eat, some do drugs, others stay in toxic relationships—we have so many ways of reacting to what's unprocessed within us. With forgiveness, we begin to slowly bring what's unprocessed to the light, where it can be processed. Unless we truly commit to the work, we're going to continue to be looped into our traumatic response cycles, unconsciously creating the conditions to stay locked in these patterns because it's where we feel safe; after all, this is the coping mechanism our mind built to protect us.

Gosh, it's no wonder people will get into relationships that remind them of the abusive parent, the verbally abusive teacher—unconsciously we enter into relationships that perpetuate the cycle of suffering because we feel safe there in the dark. I understand—it is scary to speak, write, or move the parts most hidden inside of us. We've fed and nurtured this cycle for so long, we learned to believe it's safe here in this feeling. It's not.

Until we've fully committed to this practice, to our healing and to reversing our individual cycles of suffering, we will always be dragging our past into the present and coloring the future through the filter of unprocessed trauma. Eventually this becomes a self-fulfilling prophecy where we recreate the fear and pain we felt as children in our adult relationships. This has definitely played out in my life. With a business partner, I created the same dysfunctional dynamic I had with my mom growing up. Just feel for a moment the weight of this. Imagine yourself dragging a heavy sack into every new experience. Wouldn't it be so much lighter to let it go? Let it go. We can't change the past, but we can change our relationship to it and our experience of it in the present moment.

In the trauma response cycle, the limbic system, which is responsible for balancing our moods, becomes dysregulated, and we lose our ability to self-regulate.[3] This is when problems like anxiety, depression, and sleep disorders come up. This response creates a ripple effect. We have trouble staying balanced and lose control of our internal landscape. We go from zero to 100 with no speed bumps in between, from intense emotion to shutting down. Unless we commit to healing, we will continue to seek out sex, drugs, alcohol, food, people—all of the things that, when done with fear and not love, perpetuate imbalanced states of body and mind. When we lose balance in this way, so often—I see this in my students—these behaviors play out in twos, where we'll have sex *and* do drugs, drink *and* eat—this double-trouble combo all to find some sort of relief, regulation, self-medication to make up for an out-of-whack limbic system.

I personally choose to live sober. I removed one of my most toxic means of self-medicating. It's so interesting how when you do this, at first you're faced with all of these triggers, and you've got no way to cope. You forget that the body produces its own feel-good cocktail—dopamine, serotonin, oxytocin, and endorphins—but it's a slow process to reconnect with the body's natural ways of helping you maintain happiness and calm. Endorphins are the body's natural painkiller. We produce them when we're exercising, when we listen to music, when we laugh, and of course when we meditate.[4] I want you to think about these four feel-good neurochemicals as accountability partners and healing allies.

For example, the endorphins could be someone who makes you laugh, someone who invites you to go exercise or brings you healing foods. We spark serotonin with gratitude, positive thinking, sunlight, green tea, turmeric, and fermented foods. So maybe this is your health-nerd friend who is always sending you articles about gut health (90 to 95% of serotonin is produced in the gut) and the latest food trends.[5] Dopamine is the pleasure hormone. It helps us take action and achieve goals. You can activate dopamine by setting daily and monthly measurable and achievable goals, and with a regular practice of meditation. This is the meditating friend who checks up on you and helps you meet your goals. And then we have oxytocin, the love hormone, which is released with physical contact, massage, cuddling, hugs. This healing ally is really important because it provides feelings of love and trust—exactly what we need to heal from trauma, to forgive, and for self-resolution so that we can give to the present moment the best version of ourselves.

Though they may feel unrelated, trauma and forgiveness are so interconnected. So much of our resistance to forgive stems from a very hurt and very dark place. You know what you hold. All of our stories are different. You may or may not see the ways in which trauma is running parts of your life and keeping you stuck. That's okay. The last thing I want you to do is begin to process before you're ready. This is why self-resolution is so powerful.

Blocking the Present Moment
and Blocking the Heart

I learned about forgiveness during a really difficult time in my life. I kept hearing "be present, be present," but every time I'd sit down to try to be present, my mind would remain trapped in the past, locked into feelings of how I had hurt others or others had hurt me. Guilt, remorse, and resentment were all I could hear when I sat down to "be present." Does this sound familiar? I was being the opposite of present. This was my default setting: spinning in mental agony. I did this for a long time. My forgiveness epiphany came much later, when I was able to make the connection between the stories I replayed and the fact that I had not made peace with any of them. I knew I had to make peace with my past. I needed desperately to be set free from my mistakes. I wasn't functioning because my past was totally defining me. Would forgiving absolve me of responsibility for the shit I'd done to myself and other people? No way. But it presented a way to honor what had happened and face it so a relationship with the present moment could be established. For many people, this is the block to being present, and you won't be able to know the present moment without a forgiveness practice.

It takes immense courage to make amends. As I've said, forgiveness is not something our culture values. It's brave to go against the grain, so I applaud you. Making amends doesn't mean pushing whatever it is under the rug. It doesn't mean the space it opens up will be permanent, either. This is a continuous, heart-opening practice, a way of life. Forgiveness allows room for *and*. I know I fucked up *and* I choose to move toward health and happiness. You fucked up and hurt me *and* I still wish you well. Doing this every day is like an energetic cleaning of your heart closet. It moves things out and makes space for the good shit. Feel free to make this a mantra: "I fucked up and I choose freedom. I forgive myself.

I choose freedom." Damn, doesn't that feel good to say? I just got chills. This is powerful medicine. Meaningful work simply can't take place without forgiveness.

Repeat this affirmation now: *I love the parts of myself that I'm not proud of.* Repeat it as often as you need. Feel the self-love and self-forgiveness pour into your mind—reconnecting you with the heart.

"But I Don't Have Anything or Anyone to Forgive"

Think again, honey. This is how strong the block is over your heart. Default mindset-game strong. I used to think I had nothing and no one to forgive. I remember during a thirty-day meditation retreat in Nepal, I'd look at everyone having breakdowns day after day and think, *Damn, you guys must have been some real villains out in the world before you got here* because girl, if you could have heard all the sobbing and crying going on in there, you would have thought we were in some kind of horror movie. Meanwhile, I sat on my side of the room and nothing happened. I busied myself judging everyone else for their howling and myself for having no tears. What the fuck was wrong with me? But what the fuck was wrong with *them*? Day after day, I sat with my ping-pong game of judgment—until finally I had a breakthrough. For the first time during meditation, a space opened up. Things in my life that were unprocessed started to come up. All the shit I had done to myself in reaction to how I grew up, and all the pain I had caused other people, even in small ways, began to come up. It was intense work to acknowledge all those feelings that had been hidden for so long. Before long, I joined the crying fest. I wasn't concerned with what everyone else was doing because I had my own heart to tend to. I want you to have access to that space, too, and tend to your heart. I want you to be able to hear what your heart is asking for. Take a moment to reflect in the journaling exercise below.

Write a Letter to the Motherfuckers Who Have Hurt You

On a separate piece of paper, write a letter to those who have hurt you. Make it about you. How do you feel? How has what happened affected your life? What past hurt are you carrying the remnants of today? How does what they did affect your current relationships and the way you interact with the world?

When you've finished your letter, write or repeat: *I forgive you and I wish you to be happy, healthy, and safe. May your life not be a struggle.* You don't need to send the letter; you can burn it instead.

We all have forgiveness work to do. It might not be people you need to forgive, but events, situations, entire cultures or religions. Maybe you have already done some of this work verbally, face to face. Maybe you've already made the most obvious amends to the fuckers who have hurt you. Maybe you've said you were sorry. But what remains of the energy of that pain? Where does it go? I'll tell you what, it sticks around. Anger has a way of holding on. When we go even deeper, what are the more subtle things that need our forgiveness—the energies of anger, resentment, pain, guilt? The ones that quietly hold us back. The answers to those deeper questions live in the heart. That's where the work is for all of us. It's there, and it needs your attention.

Yes, forgiveness is a big fucking deal—it takes courage, absolutely, but it's also very simple. The path of forgiveness is energetic, mental, and spiritual. It would be nice to have a face-to-face with everyone who's hurt you, but that's not the kind of forgiveness that is required. I'm talking about a letting go that is led 100% by you, internally. Forgiveness is independent; it requires nothing from another. Forgiveness work is done between you and your heart alone.

Making amends with your heart starts with self-compassion. The twin sister of self-compassion is self-forgiveness. Self-forgiveness is the path to liberation. The journaling exercise below starts to peel away the more obvious forms of forgiveness and asks you to consider yourself, too. Maybe it's time to have a talk with your heart.

Write a Letter to Yourself for What You Have Done to Hurt You

Write a letter to yourself. Get really honest. What have you done to hurt you? What do you owe yourself an apology for? Don't neglect any area of your life: go as far back as you can, through all the ages and stages you can remember.

As you start to look at the subtler forms of forgiveness that your life is needing from you, let's look further into the everyday. What kind of energy are you bringing into your days and relationships? What is the quality of your thoughts? Start to watch yourself. Are you judging yourself and others when mistakes are made? Are you carrying around any accumulation of these kinds of negative thoughts? Do you think that energy is affecting your day-to-day reality? (It definitely is.)

Judging self and others is dangerous, toxic, and not spiritually sassy. Judgment blocks spiritual progress. I learned this after judging people and being proved wrong many times, and from having false beliefs about myself along the way, like, "I'm sober; therefore I'm more enlightened than so and so . . . ," "I belong and you don't . . . ," "You drink; therefore you don't deserve enlightenment." At my "most spiritual" while monastery hopping, I'd have thoughts like these creep up. Part of my learning has been to recognize these thoughts and weed them out.

You're starting to see now why forgiveness practice is not a one-and-done activity; rather, it is an everyday affair. We can start to feel gratitude for opportunities to practice forgiveness and compassion. The practice below will help you look at what judgments and resentments you accumulate in a day. It offers a quick practice for releasing them on the spot.

Replacing Judgment

Today, pay attention to the small grudges and judgments you hold on to.

Try to notice how many there are in a day. When you multiply that by seven days, by 365 days, you can see how these small day-to-day grudges and judgments become huge trees growing in the garden of your mind, blocking your connection with your heart.

When you catch yourself, take a deep breath and say, "I forgive you."

Try to make this your new daily habit.

You've learned about how not forgiving allows resentment, fear, anxiety, and depression to run your show. But what next? How do you take your power back? Practice, practice, practice. Transforming our default ways of thinking is the key, and we do this by reinforcing new neural pathways that are rooted in forgiveness and kindness. Kindness and compassion become the new default. Repeat this now: "I commit to letting the power of forgiveness into my life."

THE POWER OF SELF-RESOLUTION

When we talk about forgiveness, we're talking about self-resolution. Self-resolution is our ability to be resolved with ourselves before we go out seeking resolution with other people. For example, when we feel hurt by somebody, we immediately want to go talk to them because we think that by talking to them, we'll find resolution. But we're actually just leaking and projecting on to the conversation and the other person. We often forget that we need to do the work from our side first. Doing the work from our side is what these forgiveness letters are. It's taking time to amend your wobbliness. When we are wobbly, we can't forgive because we are holding onto stories of the past. But when we're in our center, we can approach any situation from a place of grounded stability where the heart leads the way no matter how big or small the transgression we have made or the other person has made.

Resolving from our side is the first step toward liberation. This has worked for my students. I have so many powerful examples from students' forgiveness letters. There's one example in particular that I love. As this student and I were talking about forgiveness, she said, "I'm not interested in forgiving; it feels like I'm giving my power away. I'd rather hold a grudge." I encouraged her to try even though she had doubts. For context, this person had broken up with her partner a year prior and was still holding a grudge. The moment that she chose to open, forgive her ex, and breathe forgiveness into this exchange, a shift took place. She wrote a letter forgiving him for how he'd treated her and herself for how she'd treated herself, abandoning herself to wallow in pain for a year, and she asked forgiveness from him for the pain she'd caused. After she wrote the letter, she burned it. Keeping grudges is like drinking poison and expecting someone else to die. Self-resolution and forgiveness go hand in hand because when we learn to forgive, we are mending and releasing the hooks from the past and connecting directly to the heart. The day after she wrote this letter, she had an email from her ex checking in and asking *her* for forgiveness!

Learning to Dance with Triggers

Self-resolution has shown up in so many different ways for me. I'll share one recent example. There was a miscommunication at a Dharma Center where I was staying in Bodh Gaya during His Holiness the Dalai Lama's teachings. Someone had been very unskillful in the way they'd spoken to me. I felt really offended. I felt small and wobbly, completely off center and out of my power. I walked away from the situation and started creating all of these stories in my head about this person who had been unskillful with their words. For relief I went to the Bodhi tree. I sat there and, as I tried to forgive this person for humiliating me, I began to be able to dance with my triggers in a profoundly new way.

Yes, the way she'd spoken to me was the catalyst for my wobbly state, but my experience and my reaction were a reflection of where *I* needed work. I meditated under the Bodhi tree on forgiveness and sat with the anger, frustration, and wobbliness that came up for me, and on my own, without any help from her, I was able to forgive her for her unkind words.

Back at the center the next day, I encounter the same person. Turns out I left my bag on a bench and she was sitting there, so I couldn't avoid her. Great. So, I took the opportunity to communicate. I said, "Hey, what happened back there left a bad taste in my mouth." She said, "Oh my God, me too, I've been ruminating on it." I apologized. She said, "No, please forgive *me*, it's so out of my character, I've been so stressed out . . ." She then asked me if she could apologize to my friends, whom she had also yelled at. She found them and apologized to everyone.

This resolution wouldn't have happened if I hadn't had a little bit of clarity, having already forgiven her for how she treated me and myself for the afternoon I spent in anger, hooked and confused in this story. The lesson is: Not only does self-resolution have the power to clean up the ways you're projecting, ensuring your wounds aren't leaking onto others, but self-resolution also helps us navigate triggers in a whole new way. Self-resolution, forgiveness, and triggers all kind of go hand in hand. When we feel triggers, we're able to go inside rather than immediately going outside to blame and point fingers. We're able to go inside, notice where we're wobbly, where we need nurturing and what we need to do to come back into our center, and *only then* respond. No one can hurt you without your permission.

Triggers are part of life. Some people's presence alone might have a triggering effect on you. This can happen spontaneously, out of nowhere. This is where karma plays a role. Sometimes they don't even need to say anything to trigger you. Maybe your nervous system is out of whack, or your thoughts are all over the place, or it might be the karma you have with this particular person. Whatever it is, the only way for you to make this a lesson and learn something from it is to respond to what you feel without bringing your past into the present moment. If you feel the old fruit ripening, choose to water another seed, pick another fruit.

If you're bringing your past into the present moment, you're reacting. If you're choosing to drop your past and respond to what's coming up with clarity, compassion, and wisdom, then you are redesigning this karmic lesson, and chances are this lesson won't show up again. We will continuously learn karmic lessons because it's what we're here to do: to walk across this bridge called life until the day that we die. Throughout our walk across this bridge, we will continue to have lessons and blessings. The time will come when we can see everything as a blessing. Of course, when we're in it and it's difficult, it's very hard to see it as a lesson or as a blessing. But I have to tell you, some of the most traumatic things that ever happened to me I've been able to self-resolve to forgive and redesign the karmic lesson, and now I see them as blessings. But it takes time to do this work.

It's important to seek self-resolution before we go and speak to another person. The majority of the time, when we seek self-resolution, it's actually enough—we don't have to seek out the other person at all. When we choose self-resolution, the universe and life itself will often bring unexpected assistance. You may get a phone call, or an email might show up—something that reinforces that you have done the work. It's so beautiful when this alignment happens.

When we haven't done the self-resolution work, we leak energy and we go around unknowingly inflicting unconscious, unskillful harm onto other people. It may be very subtle, but it's impacting everything you come in contact with; it is certainly impacting the quality of your thoughts and your nervous system and everyone else's, too. That's how powerful resentment, anger, and unprocessed trauma and emotion are. Everything you're carrying in your mind becomes the filter through which you see reality. The feelings you're identifying yourself with, they're all impacting the reality outside of you as much as the reality inside of you. Self-resolution and forgiveness are foundational tools for the spiritually sassy toolbox. And it's not one-and-done work. You don't forgive once, practice self-resolution one time, and you're done. It is constant work, and these are some markers that the work is working: 1) physiologically; we have redesigned the neural pathways in the brain, recalibrating our nervous system in such a way that we have internal strength and courage to take on all of life with resilience and healthy coping skills; 2) psychologically; we have redesigned our relationship to painful memories and to our triggers, to the point that they don't always take us into a ruminating spiral; and 3) spiritually; we have gotten rid of resentment, guilt, and shameful weeds from the karmic garden of our minds, and we have redesigned our access to our heart so we can fully trust ourselves and others.

Dear Sounds True friend,

Since 1985, Sounds True has been sharing spiritual wisdom and resources to help people live more genuine, loving, and fulfilling lives. We hope that our programs inspire and uplift you, enabling you to bring forth your unique voice and talents for the benefit of us all.

We would like to invite you to become part of our growing online community by giving you three downloadable programs—an introduction to the treasure of authors and artists available at Sounds True! To receive these gifts, just flip this card over for details, then visit us at **SoundsTrue.com/Free** and enter your email for instant access.

With love on the journey,

TAMI SIMON   Founder and Publisher, Sounds True

sounds true
many voices, one journey   800.333.9185

ST33C

SAY "BYE, GIRL" TO PAIN AND MEAN IT

Forgiveness is an active practice, something that must be done over and over again until the relationship to the event, the story, the thing—transforms. Until *you* transform. Step two of this work is just the beginning of your transformation. It's not as if you do a forgiveness practice once, or you read this chapter, and then you easily say "bye, girl" to all the pain of the past, and all of the hurt you've caused yourself and others gets wiped away. No. It's not a one-time deal; it's a constant practice. Instead of being completely hooked and dragged by the stories, you're able instead to notice them and sprinkle the forgiveness glitter on them as they arise. You're constantly redirecting the mind toward the heart: sprinkle, sprinkle.

There will come a time when you'll pick up the book—the one that contains all your lack of forgiveness for yourself and other people, and the shitty feelings that come with it—and you'll be able to close that book and put it back on the shelf. You'll always have access to the book, but it won't be your default anymore. It won't define you. Instead, you'll start to see from a new perspective, from your new story. The book will always be authored by you, but it will no longer define the present-moment you. Your new story will be of how you've transmuted the pain, how you've turned traumatic events and heartaches into freedom. Default mode is done. You are the hero.

Forgiveness is so powerful because it allows choice where there was none. Most of us are living without choice. Painful memories arise and you're totally taken by them. They become your day, your week, or, if you're like me, they become your years.

When we look into our spiritual toolbox, or what I like to call our spiritual fanny pack, compassion grows and becomes a resource. Practicing forgiveness increases our capacity to be compassionate and build what the

Buddha called merit. Accumulating virtuous merit purifies your karmic garden. We can look at merit as spiritual money that is used to pay karmic debt—much like accumulating "points," but with the idea that the credit your virtuous deeds earns you is greater happiness in this life and beyond. Practicing forgiveness and compassion builds your karmic credit, so to speak.

∽

Below is a combined breathing and mantra practice that aids in the letting-go process and also helps to call in all kinds of goodness. The breath gives us space to infuse painful memories with healing words, creating a supportive internal vocabulary.

Meditation: I Am Worthy

Breathing in, say to yourself, *I am worth the effort.*

Breathing out, say to yourself, *I am allowing myself to heal.*

Breathing in: *I am worth the effort.*

Breathing out: *I am allowing myself to forgive.*

Breathing in: *I am worth the effort.*

Breathing out: *I am allowing myself to let go.*

Breathing in: *I am worth the effort.*

Breathing out: *I am allowing myself to love.*

Breathing in: *I am worth the effort.*

Breathing out: *I am allowing myself to be loved.*

Breathing in: *I am worth the effort.*

Breathing out: *I am allowing myself to shine.*

Breathwork is a way for you to release the tension that comes up each time a memory arises that you haven't been able to forgive or make amends with. When we get hooked in a story, the breath becomes shallow, blood starts pumping through the body, and we go into fight/flight/freeze mode. When we're there, we can't forgive ourselves or anyone; we can't even connect to reality. When we do breathwork as a core practice, we gain the ability to notice when we've become hooked in a story, and we can use the breath to diffuse the emotional charge of the story—not in order to put it under the rug again, but to have enough space to be with the feeling and forgive it so we can move on. Each time you are in deep connection with the breath, when a traumatic memory arises, a new perspective opens up and an old shackle is released.

Breathwork Practice

This is a powerful breathing technique that can help anyone learn how to breathe properly, by using our diaphragm, commonly known as belly breathing. Most people breathe incorrectly, using only the muscles in the chest, which indicates that they are emotionally guarded.

This practice, which is also taught in the military, helps to reduce anxiety by bringing relaxation to mind and body and balancing the heart rate. It can be done lying down, standing, or seated.

- Breathe in long, from the lower abdomen and diaphragm through the back of the throat, for four seconds.

- Hold for four seconds.

- Breathe out slowly through the back of the throat for six seconds.

- Hold empty for two seconds.

Do this for five minutes.

MORE TO PRACTICE

Remember we talked about trauma and resentment (the effects of not forgiving) hanging around in your body? One way to start moving that out is . . . to move. Below are some ideas to get you moving with the specific intention of aiding in your forgiveness practice.

Time to Move

Forgiveness Dance

Stop what you're doing, put on some music, and dance it out. As you move, sync with these words: "I am willing to forgive." Set the intention that this joyful movement be in service of your healing, specifically to welcoming forgiveness into your life where it's needed. Dance off resentments, regrets, guilt, anger—anything you need to release. Dance as if no one is watching. Try to move every part of your body.

Hip Openers: Pigeon Pose and Frog

These *asanas*, or postures, are mega hip openers. Do this when you feel at a loss (like my moment in retreat when everyone was having breakthroughs but me). Use these when you feel you need to go deeper in order to heal. We keep emotions stored in our tight hips, and when we open them, things can be revealed to us that were previously hidden. Do these regularly to keep things open and flowing.

Movement is not the only external way to support healing. Let's not neglect what we put into our bodies in the form of food. Is your food nourishing you or keeping you blocked? Below are some tips for emotionally supporting your body as you do this deep work. Physical health supports spiritual progress.

Feeding the Heart

As you nourish yourself today or this week, cook with forgiveness as the intention. Truly any mundane act can be a meditation. When you sit down to eat, bless your meal and ask that it help set you free. Ask that it support your healing. Make it part of your heart revolution. Repeat the intention: "This meal is unshackling me from my past."

You can also:

- Dedicate your meal to someone.

- Add turmeric, nature's natural antidepressant, whenever possible.

Commit to making forgiveness a new way of life for you and watch the magic happen. Now that you understand what forgiveness is and the power in it, it's yours to use as often as you like. It should be a staple in your new toolbox.

Now, onto writing the new story of you. Honey, you're ready.

5

The New Story of You

Step 3: Spray spiritual bleach on the belief systems that have kept you stuck.

So, who are you? Not your labels, but You. Deep down. You being a sister or a brother or a daughter or a son or a worker or a gay man or a trans woman or a black woman or a student or an immigrant or . . . I mean, who are you according to your heart? What are your deeper qualities? What are the textures of your deeper being? And what do you want? Not materially. I don't care about your monetary or social or romantic goals. What does your heart want? Not in a romantic sense. What are the needs of your heart? How does your heart want to be expressed? Do you know? Does the question freak you out? Piss you off? Like, WTF is this guy talking about? (I'm smiling at you, relax.) In this chapter we'll be exploring the deeper layers of you. I'll give you a hint: your heart is central to dismantling your false beliefs and getting to the true essence of you.

I had my first meeting with my essence on my first trip to India. I was doing something called a death meditation, and I had a powerful psychological response to it. There was nothing inherently sacred about me being in India. Going to India is not a requirement, but what it offered me was the first space I'd ever had to *really* meet myself, and the message I had for me hit me like a ton of bricks: "Sah, you have so much work to do." I had been trapped in my stories, and for the first time I could see some glimmer of truth. Perhaps everything I'd been told was a lie. Perhaps straight-up everything I thought I knew was a lie. I felt in those moments how out of alignment my thoughts were with who I was. They simply did not fit the way I wanted to feel. They did not match who I was beginning to see I was, in my heart.

YOUR LIFE, YOUR STORY, YOUR CHOICE

So, this story of you—what you do, who you are, what your potential is, your worth, your passion, your work, what you care about, your pain, your traumas, what your hobbies are, what you're good at, what you're not good at, where you come from, who you come from—most of what you deem you is conditioned or absorbed from your environment and society. Only a tiny sliver is the real You, and it is your work to open the door more and more for that sliver to expand and your full light to shine. Each time you make the choice to turn off autopilot—where you're playing and replaying all the stories that have kept you stuck—you are allowing yourself to be more fully who you really are, and your true, uninhibited personality can shine.

Who you really are. It's not as esoteric or mystical as it may sound, as if the person beneath the bullshit was a magical unicorn or something. No, it's much simpler. Which is key. So often we're looking for this big aha moment or breakthrough when what we've been searching for—*you*—has been here all along. The innate qualities of the nonjudgmental, loving observer, the wisdom that arises when you have knowing or intuition: it is right there between your breath. That's it, folks. That's the You I want you to get to know. Who you are is the essence of your heart, a creative genius and unconditionally loving and courageous as fuck. The mind is your vehicle to uncover this part of yourself.

You, Full Power

Okay, so this is gonna sound edgy—but I know you are ready to hear it! Have you ever been around someone who is not living in their full power, who is so not expressed from their heart, who is so on autopilot? It can be suffocating to watch. First things first, we don't judge, because if we do, we are watering the seeds of judgment in our karmic garden. We don't write them off either, because again you are watering and planting those vicious tendencies in your garden. But what we *do* need to do, for everyone's sake, is realize how you will convey the language of your heart into the world—how you will express compassion, joy, wisdom, and love, so that when you enter a room full power, it's nonverbally communicated that everyone can let their hair down, they can take off the mask, and they can let the freak flag fly. Our work is to tame our neuroses, to train our mind, to weed our karmic garden so we can use the powerhouse energy of the mind to find our own, unique way of expressing our innate qualities from the heart as our gift to the world. This is where your own unique, fabulous personality comes out and stays out. Everyone, please welcome your inner mega boss.

You are here on Earth to engage with the world, to use your body, to develop your unique personality as an extension and expression of your heart. In chapter 1 I told you about how I once thought the ascetic path was the way, but I have since found that the Me I am called to be is full power. Part of my work is to embrace all parts of me: the quiet observer that is with me all the time, as I meditate and breathe, as well as the laughing, dancing, vital human man I am. This is my magic. This body I was given, this personality, this mind, this heart—this is my magic. So this is where the magic happens, where the unique and beautiful person you were meant to be (which you already are, underneath it all) can bloom and share your heart with the world through the wonderful vessel that is you. Dang, girl. Ram Dass said, "I would like my life to be a statement of love and compassion—and where it isn't, that's where my work lies."[1] On the sassy path, we go courageously, full power, into that work and those lessons.

What covers over and inhibits this full expression of you are your stories. We have to stop hiding our magic behind our stories. We're so afraid of being looked at as the freak, the weirdo, as an "other." But I have to tell you, honey, the more of a freak weirdo I became, the more I stood in my power, the more I stepped into my abundance, the more people wanted to be around me and hear what I had to say.

Rewriting your story to match your essence is what you came here to do. We are here to create from our pain; we are here to transcend the ways we've been hooked; we are here to transmute and transform our sorrows, guilt, and shame into something that will help liberate others, including the people who will come after us.

Cleaning House Inside and Out

When I say "rewriting your story," I'm going back to a core Buddhist principle that says we are both totally interdependent and utterly impermanent. Who we are right now depends on our relationship to what's in front of us, what's around us, and what's activating our senses. How is your environment being processed by your mind and impacting your reality? Who we are now is completely different from who we will be tomorrow. What's around you directly influences your reality; what's around you, and your relationship to what's around you, *are* the conditions that support your present moment. While these conditions don't define your heart, they do influence the quality of your mind. Therefore your environment is either getting you closer to the heart or further from it. The way your essence expresses itself is unique to your particular karma. The most important, and also the simplest, thing you can do is commit to planting and nurturing the seeds that support the reality you want.

For example, who you hang out with is who you become. As we are cleaning up our internal landscape, we also have to have the courage to clean up our external lives.

Maybe you've never left home. Maybe you've been living in the same town you grew up in because that's what everybody did. Maybe, as you're reading this, it's time to get the fuck out of your hometown. Maybe it's time to go to the big city, or maybe it's time to explore the part of you that's curious, that always wanted to try something new. Remember, honey: if you choose to live the same life seventy-five years in a row, you're going to arrive at the last breaths of your life with regret that you didn't get out there. I actually hear this all the time, especially when I return from traveling—people say, "I'm gonna do that when I retire." And I go, "Bitch, do you even know *if* you're gonna be around to retire and travel the world?" Stop following this norm! This constructed idea of safety is not making you safe; it's making you more insecure, more fearful, more doubtful—it's keeping you away from your heart, away from the potential you have to be out of the spiritual closet and deeply in the now. You wouldn't have the wish in your heart if it wasn't meant for you. Stop being so afraid to claim that wish. Be in the heart. Create with courage—create something, but also, create your life. How do you want to live?

Redefining Success

When we talk about rewriting the story of you, it's important we realize that we all have an individual mission here on Earth. There's a 99% chance that you are trying to accomplish goals set not by you, but by your parents, your grandparents, and society. I'm 99.9% sure that you have no definition of success for yourself.

The beautiful thing about stripping away the noise and bullshit until there's only the essential you left is You get to decide. You get to choose. You get to create new definitions. This is the first step in the new story. *Success* is such a loaded word. What it means to each individual depends on their own story. Your definition of success may be attached to proving someone wrong or remaining rooted in shame or living out someone else's vision for you. Think about what success means to you and write down your definition. Be really specific. Really envision yourself successful. What are you doing? Who are you with? What do you look like? What do you have?

Now I want you to focus on how you feel. How does success *feel*? That feeling is the real definition of success. Likely it is the same feeling as joy. And what is that for you? Calm? At peace? In alignment? What is it? That, my friend, is success. If you can feel that way, you are on your way.

When you need a success reality check, you can ask yourself a few questions to help you snap back. Let's try it on a goal. This should be something external that you want to achieve.

What do you want?

_____

Who taught you to want this?

_____

Do you still want it?

_____

Now try it with a belief. You can go back to page 57 and remind yourself of some of the negative ones you've been carrying with you.

What do you believe?

_____

Who taught you to believe this?

_____

Do you still believe it?

_____

When in doubt, focus on the feeling. If you can feel success, feel joy, as you define it, you are free. It is possible to become your reality.

ALL ABOUT YOU

As you are learning, _You_ is a complicated being, a complicated story. If you are to write a new story of you, you must first become the expert in all things you. As you now know, awareness is power. If you can identify it, you can change it. It's when we live on autopilot that we lose our power.

On a separate piece of paper or in your journal, answer the following questions, spending five minutes or less on each. Don't overthink, just let it flow.

1. What is the story of you? (In other words, if you had to write a story of your life with a beginning, a struggle/conflict, a climax, and an ending, all the way to now, how would that story go?)

2. How has your story/your past shaped you?

3. Has any one (or more) traumatic event or memory informed how you think about yourself?

4. What has been the biggest struggle of your life?

5. What has been the biggest gift of your life?

6. What does success mean to you?

7. Who are you grateful for?

8. What about yourself are you most grateful for?

9. What are you most proud of?

10. What are you most ashamed of?

11. Who are you in this moment?

12. How have you changed?

13. What do you love about you?

14. What do you wish you could change about you?

15. What do you wish you could change about your life?

16. What is your deepest wish for you and your life? (Forget about any perceived limitations—wish big!)

The mind is powerful (as we know) and sneaky (it makes us believe we *are* our thoughts and feelings). Now that you have an understanding of what your inner critic is and that it's pretty much always going—and usually biased toward the negative—look at what you wrote and ask yourself, for each response:

Which words/responses were those of the inner critic/habituated mind?

Which words/responses are your heart?

Now look at what you've written. Ask yourself: What is true? Circle the true words and sentences.

HAVE YOUR HEART'S BACK

All this time, you've had your mind's back. You've been loyal to your untrained mind, which unintentionally does *not* have your best interests in mind. When it's narrating your emotions and daily life events, having random opinions, convincing you you're nothing, talking you out of doing the things that are scary but necessary for your growth—you've been so loyal! Meanwhile, your heart is all, "Hello? Is anyone listening?" It's time to give it the attention it deserves. Your heart believes in you and contains the wisdom you need to make courageous steps forward in your life. Remember, your heart is where your goodness lies. So how does this muscle grow if you've been accustomed to abiding every whim of the inner critic your whole life?

A beautiful and profound way to lock in with the spiritual heart is for you to visualize your in and out breaths as coming from the center of your chest. Remember, the doorway to the spiritual heart is at the heart itself. Here's a practice to help you reconnect to the heart field.

Heart Visualization

Visualize your in and out breaths coming from the center of your chest.

Take a deep breath in for a count of four, visualizing it coming in from the spiritual heart, and hold it there for two seconds.

And then breathe out for six seconds.

Repeat this practice for a few minutes, continuing to visualize the breath coming from the center of the chest.

Heart Goals vs. Mind Goals

We've been talking a lot about who you are. But, what is it that you want? This question often gets lost in our mind's desires. "I want to buy a house. I want to get married. I want success." Heart goals are something different. They are the force of the initial wish for anything—the intention behind the goal. Intentions are heart messages. Getting clear on our own will help us speak the language of the heart. The mind, because of all its conditioning, has become polarized and untrained, so the wishes that come from this untrained place are selfish and lead us to more suffering. When you train the mind to support the music in your heart, you'll know exactly what to do.

Write down five of your goals below.

Mind Goal	Heart Goal
Ex. Find love	Experience greater and more intimate connection
Be successful at work	Do work that helps the awakening of my community
1. _____	1. _____
2. _____	2. _____
3. _____	3. _____
4. _____	4. _____
5. _____	5. _____

These heart goals are your new goals. When you find yourself wanting something, reaching for something, ask yourself: What is behind this want? Remember, karma starts with intention. There is information within our wishes, but they often need to be unpacked so we can see them in their purest state.

Talking Back

Write five of the most common things your inner critic says to you on the left side. On the right side, write what your heart would say.

Inner Critic Talk

Heart Talk

Ex. You will probably fail

Nothing's stopping me from succeeding

1. _____

1. _____

2. _____

2. _____

3. _____

3. _____

4. _____

4. _____

5. _____

5. _____

This is your new self-talk. Empower yourself with statements like these and they will become your new default. Action starts with thoughts. If you can think differently, then you are on your way to changing your life.

THE TRUTH OF WHO YOU ARE

This is the big secret that I hope doing the above exercise has shown you: You are good and kind and worthy and beautiful and loving and compassionate. That is what you're made of at your core. You are exactly who your heart knows you are. You can trust that. Everything else is a story. As we tap into the awareness and knowledge of this innate goodness and become comfortable with this truth, more and more each day, this goodness muscle gets stronger. As the goodness muscle grows, guess what starts to get quieter? The inner fucking critic, because it loses its power. It's still talking a mile a minute about whatever negative shit, but you are up here, tapped into your innate goodness, saying back to it, "Nah, we're good."

Thirteen Ways to Update Your Hardware

1. Zap a negative thought with a good thought.
2. Practice gratitude.
3. Meditate and do breathwork.
4. Check in with your inner world often.
5. Say kind things to yourself.
6. Hang out with inspiring people.
7. Be yourself to the max.
8. Don't gossip.
9. Practice nonviolence with words and actions (and no killing, not even a mosquito).
10. Acknowledge when you're wrong and admit mistakes.
11. Tell the truth always.
12. Act with heart integrity.
13. Move your body regularly.

Make a Heart Wish

A few pages back I asked you to write down your deepest wish for you and your life. How has that wish changed? Are there any questions you need to ask of this wish? Do you need to know its intention? With all of this in mind, and making any necessary edits, write your wish for you and your life below. Creating the optimal conditions for you to align with and receive this wish is what our work will be in the following chapters.

My wish for my life and myself: _____

_____

Before We Move On

If only we knew that thoughts are simply passing by us and not originating from us. Our minds are like radio antennas picking up and processing everything that's passing by. The problem is, we believe all of the thoughts our minds are processing as indicators of truth, when the real indicator of truth is beneath all the thoughts. Beneath your thoughts is where you have access to the present moment, where you can hear the heart. Instead of getting caught up in thoughts, you relearn how to lead with the heart-based impulse of love, wisdom, compassion, and joy. When this impulse of the heart is nurtured and practiced, it will lead you toward creativity, uninhibited self-expression, and courage. But it will take work to continuously redesign our impulses since so many of them are cluttered and mixed with destructive feelings, unkind thoughts, and unresolved trauma.

Thoughts and feelings will arise without any help from you, and it is your job to choose to believe these thoughts and feelings as indicators of truth or choose to free yourself. We'll continue to learn little ways to support the new (true) you. The idea is that eventually you will believe your innermost being and create conditions to replenish and nurture yourself until you have become completely awakened in this lifetime. Does that feel good to say or what?

Be Your
Own Guru

Step 4: Wake up your
inner wisdom.

This step is about awakening to our innermost dreams and
wishes, our inner knowing: those dreams that have been
placed in our hearts that we've been too afraid to say out
loud, or even to ourselves. I'm talking about those. I'm
talking about learning to hear the inner knowing that will
guide you through each decision on your journey to the
life of your dreams, to your purpose in this life, every day.
It's time to wake up, activate, and start making choices and
receiving the guidance that supports your best life. The
days of ignoring your callings are over. You're on your way
to becoming a master manifester. You've got to tap into
your inner compass and get out of your own way. In the
last chapter, you revealed your deepest wish to yourself.
Now go get it.

Well, okay: there's more to unpack first. What is the
intention behind this wish? How does it connect you to
your unique life purpose? How does it connect you more
deeply to your heart? How does it help others? And finally,
what are the steps to making it your reality? Deep down, I

believe you know what's good for you. That's the wisdom you will learn to follow to get closer to the life you have the potential to live. This is where the magic happens.

THE ROLE OF PURPOSE

Purpose is the prerequisite for manifesting the life of your dreams. Living in your purpose is the fastest way to purify your karma. You have begun to understand the importance of cleaning up your mind and resolving mental obscurations and delusions. You have begun to introduce practices that support the awakening of your heart. And you have begun to learn the language of the heart and how to pick up on its cues. How beautiful, how powerful that you now have this discernment! These are your most important tools; this is your inner wisdom.

Now it's time to find your purpose and gift it back into the world—this is the cocktail for a purposeful, meaningful, passionate life. Without purpose, we're on a journey but we don't know why. We've got these beautiful, magical tools inside of us, but we don't know for what purpose to use them. We're crossing the bridge, but we have no idea why, or what it's leading to. We can't have true awakening without the full body knowing of where we are going and *why*.

When in Doubt, Get Curious

Curiosity is the pathway to purpose. It is crucial to allow it, make space for it, and follow it. It is yet another way the heart speaks to you. What are you pulled toward? What are you naturally drawn to do, without any shoulds or being told? What do you find so interesting you do it on your days off? Tapping into your own curiosities is the first step.

My curiosity led me to healing work. It began when I was still working in fashion. In no way was I in alignment yet with my purpose, but the seeds had been planted, and I had a real interest in healing that led me to want to learn about all things spiritual and wellness-related. Even before I hit rock bottom and lost my business, things on the outside seemed to be going well for me—I was outwardly successful—but on the inside suffering was tugging at me constantly. Something was whispering to me that I needed to heal and that my work in the fashion industry was not my path to freedom. I was using drugs and drinking at that time, and only now, as I live a sober life, can I see clearly that I was using drugs and alcohol to suppress, tame, and medicate the deep suffering I was experiencing. I was recovering from my own unprocessed trauma—we are all doing this in some way or another; being human is recovering from unprocessed trauma—and drugs and alcohol were the tools I unskillfully used to cope until I finally broke down. Only then, having no idea what else to do, did I allow myself to follow my innermost curiosity. Eventually, this led me to dedicate my life to finding sustainable tools to heal myself.

Following my curiosities, I started to redesign my relationship to my traumatic memories and learn what it is to get in contact with my heart. I remember during my time at the fashion magazine, in the little free time I had, I was constantly researching spirituality and world religion and wanting to go to talks and events and workshops. I studied Kabbalah for a while. Maybe I was interested in it on a superficial level because Madonna was into it at the time and would even be at the Kabbalah Center where I briefly practiced. But maybe it was because I had a genuine curiosity. Curiosity is not random. I think we forget that the things we are curious about are the things that will set us free.

Ever notice how you have an unlimited capacity for what your curiosity draws you to? Unlike the work you don't love, which exhausts and burns you out after not much time, for the things you are truly curious about, there seems to be a limitless well of energy you can tap into. This is the magic of it all. This is how you know it is heart guidance. This has been true for me, anyway.

Once I got out of breakdown mode and entered breakthrough mode, I was following my curiosity full-time. Doing this was like nothing else I had ever committed to. I had an enormous amount of energy for it—I could go on retreat after retreat after retreat, to workshops, to talk after talk, and never tire. I was so hungry for knowledge, and I was finding that it fed me fully. As a result, I had limitless energy. And the moment I became sober, I had even more energy to do research and watch talks and read books and talk to people. Following these passions was what was really setting me free. I realized that curiosity had become my work, and that I could do this all the time. I not only *could*, but I *wanted* to do this all the time.

There is a logic to all of this magic. The thing I've realized about my life purpose is that when I followed the things I was innately curious about, I had a constant internal replenishment, a well of energy and power to find out more and keep building and connecting things in a deep way. You can have this same experience as a student or in your job. You are learning and making connections in the mind. When we connect things in the mind, the brain recognizes that there is a pattern being created, and dopamine shows up. When there's dopamine, a feel-good chemical cocktail is cooked up inside of us, giving us a boost of energy to help us work toward our goal. As we're accomplishing goals, dopamine shows up again. This is the scientific way of understanding this self-fulfilling process. The spiritual way of understanding it is that curiosity is your heart asking you to discover it. How beautiful is that? Your curiosity is one beautiful way your heart speaks to you.

Finding Your Curiosity
(adapted from Steven Kotler)[1]

On a separate piece of paper or in your journal, write down a list of twenty-five things you're curious about.

Be specific. For example, it's not enough to be curious about, say, plants. Go deeper. What is it about plants? If it's mushrooms you find fascinating, try to go deeper still. If you research, for example, you will find that mushrooms were used to dye fabric before the invention of synthetic dyes. If it's mental illnesses that makes you curious, go deeper. Is it depression in particular? A curiosity about depression might lead you to want to understand the human mind. You will start to learn these things as you dive deeper into your curiosities.

So, you'll need to spend some time writing down your curiosities. When you're finished, I want you to look for and highlight patterns. Look at where three or even four things come together and connect under one umbrella. How do all of the things that interest you relate to one another?

Most people find it difficult to identify twenty-five things, so take your time and know this will take a while. Don't be afraid. Do this with curiosity. Try not to share until you have internalized these curiosities.

Personal Fulfillment + Helping Others = Lit Purpose

I knew I was living my purpose the moment I realized that what was truly bringing me fulfillment was helping other people. The moment we figure out how we can help others while also following our passion and curiosity is the moment passion becomes purpose. Life purpose has to do with the things you're curious about, yes. But without a big-picture connection to a greater good beyond yourself, our curiosities lack depth. Your curiosities become your passion and your passion becomes your purpose. How? When you are helping others.

I want to paint a little picture of how my curiosity led to my passion, and how I started to see signs that what I was interested in was leading me to help others. I didn't label it this way back then, but thinking back, even when I was working in fashion, I would find myself having these spiritual conversations with the talents we were shooting. I remember styling a very high-profile celebrity for the magazine. That day, as I styled her, I remember having a conversation with her about the human condition. Later this celebrity tweeted about our conversation, and I was so struck that what we'd discussed and my insights had made an impact on her.

That was one of the very first messages I received from my heart about my ability to connect with people on psychological and spiritual levels. This has become my gift. When you start sharing your gifts is when the magic happens. So, please don't keep your gifts to yourself! You are losing out, and the world is, too. When I started to share and teach, I received this divine feedback that assured me, "Oh, okay, I'm on the right path." We have to pay attention to the internal and external signs. Part of this is your inner well getting full. Do you feel blissed out? Pay attention to the way your body responds. Oftentimes, your body will give you signs that it feels in tune or out of whack. Listen.

When I started to research my curiosities, I found a language that was not part of the vocabulary of the circles I was in. Every time I would bring up an idea, people would be so interested in what I was talking about. Again, the seeds of the message I would eventually hear loud and clear: people want tools to heal, so if you have them, share. Once you realize what you're curious about, chances are it'll be something that will help other people. That, my love, is the sweet spot I want for you.

I began to travel, to learn from many different teachers. I became a sponge soaking up all the knowledge and wisdom I could. I was floundering, searching for something after two failed business ventures, and I didn't know what to do. Faced with the depression and trauma I'd avoided my whole life, I filled my empty self with wisdom and tried to learn what I could about the human condition so I could start to feel better. With my studies and travels, I created an arsenal of tools. I was on a healing path, and my life was transforming. I was building a new life. The natural next step was to share. We hear this so often: fill your cup and then you can help fill the cups of others.

The first time I shared some of the tools that had helped me was when I was living at a retreat center. As I shared, I had a real aha moment. Something hit me, like, "Wow, I really *am* meant to be doing this." Until then, I was trapped in the limiting belief that I had to make money before I could live my purpose. I didn't realize that I could make money doing what I love, doing what I was curious about. I am continuously seeking to learn and develop more, grow more, heal more. The more I transform my internal world, the more I can help other people, and the more I help other people, the more my inner world is transformed. It's such a beautiful, sustainable cycle. This is my mission.

CONNECTING TO PURPOSE AND MISSION

People who are living a life of purpose often have a sense of urgency about their life. It's not a rush mindset, but a heightened awareness about all that needs to be done in the world for all people to be happy and for everyone to be deeply connected to their hearts and living their purpose (no pressure!). These people are not complacent—they are fierce enough to make change, and they are tired of suffering and feeling like shit. Living on purpose is living the high vision. We are either living the high vision or no vision.

Living a life of purpose is directly related to an awareness of how much suffering there is in the world. Seeing this suffering, you are inspired and driven to be of service. But I want to clarify something really important. It doesn't matter what you do. For example, you don't have to start an NGO. You could be making sculptures, and if you're making sculptures with the intention of expressing your fierceness, for example, when someone looks at your work, it will be an invitation to feel what you felt. You can be an accountant, and if you're creating Excel spreadsheets and you're plugging in numbers but you're doing it all with joy, this can set you free just as much as meditation can. And when someone looks at the spreadsheet you created, this is the message they are going to receive. It doesn't matter what you do; it just matters that you do it with joy and intention. You could be a barista or an editor or an architect. Are you putting love, joy, and intention into what you're doing? No matter who you are or what resources you have or where you are in your life, you can do anything, big or small, with the intention to help others. This is tantra. This is using real life to get free and free others.

Finding Your Mission

On a separate piece of paper, write down a list of fifteen things you want solved in the world.

Try to get very, very granular about this. You can't say "world peace" or "world hunger." We need to get more specific. For example, "I want to help solve the food desert in the Bronx," or "I want to be able to help with homelessness in the East Village," or "I want to help addicts on skid row."

When you're done writing your list, it's time to figure out how the things that came together on your list of curiosities connect to your list of things you want solved.

I want you to study and research those intersections. Just by doing this exercise, you're positioning yourself more profoundly in your own, powerful, creative, beautiful way of relating to your interests. You can begin to nurture your curiosities so much that they become your passion, and passion will inspire your purpose.

Your homework is to research your intersections for fifteen minutes every day for the next two weeks. Try not to share your lists or this process or your findings with anyone just yet. Only share after the two weeks are completed. When we share something vulnerable too soon, people who are not living their purpose may discourage us or tell us we're wrong. Sometimes they can do this with body language alone. This might be your best friend or your parent or your lover. It's unintentional. For people who are not living their purpose, you sharing about your purpose can be triggering, and their reactions may pivot you away from what you came here to do. Hold your cards close and protect what you care about, especially in the early stages.

After two weeks, you can start sharing with people if you feel moved to, because by then you'll have enough experiential understanding of your findings; it won't just be intellectual.

The beautiful thing is that once you realize that the things you're curious about can fulfill you *and* help others, you understand that you're not only helping yourself to be free, you're helping everybody else to be free, too. Try to let go of the fear that you won't be able to make a living. This is unknown, but the anxiety of it is enough to kill even the seed of a dream before it has time to grow. Believe you can make a sustainable living doing something fulfilling that you enjoy. This belief is part of the natural law of abundance you must tap into.

Connecting Your Life Experience
to Your Purpose

Make a list of three things you've overcome. For me it was addiction, anxiety, and depression.

Then answer the following questions.

1. How did you overcome?

2. What helped/what was the antidote?

3. Where are you now?

The obstacles you've faced and overcome will give you information about what your mission might be and the impact you have the potential to make. Look back on your lists of curiosities and intersections. Depending on your challenge, maybe your story will lead you to work with people who have mental illness. This will be personal to you.

Purpose and Flow

So, you're doing what you're curious about, you're following it up with what you wish to be solved in the world, you're training the mind, you're figuring out how you want to give back, you're gaining access to the language of the heart—these things create the conditions for you to access the flow state. Flow is a high-performing state of mind where complete *knowing* takes over logical thinking. Do you ever surprise yourself as you're speaking aloud or writing? Where you're like, "Damn, bitch, that was good!" That's flow. In this state, the conditioned mind drops away, wisdom emerges, and there is complete immersion in what you're doing. Generally we find flow when we're doing something of great purpose to us.

The flow state is one of the most powerful states we can achieve. From a chemical perspective, these neurochemicals are involved in your flow state: adrenaline (energy), dopamine (reward), endorphins (pleasure), and anandamide (bliss and lateral thinking).[2] Anandamide is a lesser-known neurochemical and helps us think laterally, beyond logic.

You can recognize flow by its texture. You may remember times when you've been so focused it felt like an out-of-body experience. When you are in flow, you're not hungry, you're not tired, and internal chatter falls away. Some people call it being "in the zone." In Buddhism it's called *samadhi*. Flow happens when we become our action, our intent, and there is a feeling of union.

When you're tapped into flow, synchronicities become more common. There is spontaneous correspondence between the inner and outer world, which helps you connect to the universe at large. We're experiencing an expression of the part of us that is already completely awakened.

The following are some natural ways for you to tap into the flow state.

- Turn your passion into your purpose.
- Participate in high-performance sports.
- Meditate.
- Do yoga.
- Take social risks (such as going out on a limb to meet someone new).
- Be generous.
- Help others.

MANIFESTATION AND ABUNDANCE AS A WAY OF LIFE

The word "manifestation" gets thrown around so often that even when I say it aloud, I'm usually like, "Ugh, whatever," because it gives the impression that creating the life you want doesn't require effort. It *does* require a lot of skillful effort, including practicing supportive habits and rituals that set you free enough for you to get to know what you are really here to do, your mission. "Manifesting" is simply another word for the work of building supportive habits, people, places, and things into your life so you can live to your fullest potential.

We all have an individual mission, and we all have the power to manifest the life of our dreams. Eastern philosophies say we are back here to accomplish the missions we didn't finish in our last life. How cool is that?! You could also ignore that, if it's too far out for you, and stick with the understanding that in this lifetime, you have a unique mission and individual way of going about the world. And this individual way of going about the world can be an invitation for everyone that meets you to awaken their mission within themselves, too.

To be honest with you and open up to a vulnerable place, I didn't know I really had a mission until recently. I started working in the fashion industry because my parents had a clothing company when I was growing up in Brazil, and when I moved to LA, all I knew was how to manipulate clothes in a way that looked inspiring for other people. But deep down I didn't realize I was hooked on superficial aspects of the fashion industry that weren't setting me free. I'm not saying that fashion is superficial, but the way I was approaching it was. I was insecure and looked for belonging by dressing and acting a certain way. I didn't have a sense of belonging within me, in my heart. The foundational needs of my heart weren't replenished enough, so I sought to replenish them outside of myself. But remember: we have to replenish our basic heart needs from within ourselves so that we don't require external gratification. Only then do we create a sustainable loop of supportive and skillful ways of replenishing ourselves. This allows us to step more and more into a life of abundance.

It wasn't until a couple of years ago that I started making a living doing what I love. Until very recently, I still had shame and fear around money. Why? Because deep down I didn't feel worthy of making money doing what I loved.

Flow. Abundance. These were both trigger words for me until very recently. I opened my first savings account only last year, and I still don't have a credit card. And although I am making a lot of money doing what I love and traveling around the world and sharing and teaching, it's a constant process of deconditioning the generations and generations of scarcity mindset that I unconsciously subscribed to (we'll discuss scarcity mindset more in chapter 8).

Most likely all of us are familiar with the mindset that you have to struggle to be happy, you have to struggle to live your dreams, and you have to struggle to manifest abundance. It's not true. Struggle is not required. We need to redesign this default so we can create skillful rituals that will set us free. We need to wake up to the fact that we have the potential to create a life of abundance, a life of flow, a life where we can be living our dreams every day—a life where we are in a constant state of awe and surprise, and spontaneity becomes the default for us. How often are you spontaneous? How often are you actually tapping into the flow?

I'm talking about a slightly different kind of flow now. This kind of flow is not a mental state but a way of life. It's the opposite of struggle. This kind of flow stems from a place of believing you're worth it. You have a baseline belief in yourself and your dreams, and you have faith that you will create the life you are working toward. That is life in flow. It is a way of being that not only supports manifestation, but is the embodiment of manifestation. This way of being is not spiritual bypassing in that it doesn't mean you're not making an effort; rather, it means you have fierce self-belief as a guiding force and you *believe* good things can happen to you. You carry no doubt that what you're working toward may fail. And if it does, you have the skills to pick yourself up and remind yourself once again that you're worth it.

This is something I have struggled with. When talk of money and abundance becomes real and opportunities start flowing to you, then the real tests come. Sometimes, it's when you get what you asked for that the most challenging work begins. When you get what you want is often when imposter syndrome sets up shop in the mind, a new and sneaky form of negative self-talk. "Who the fuck do you think you are?" "No, no, no, no, no, *you* don't make this kind of money." "You're in over your head." "Are you crazy? You can't do this!" "You are a FRAUD!" As you start to reap the rewards of your hard work, as your dreams start to manifest, you will need to daily unhook this motherfucker, imposter syndrome, because growth is scary. Yet growth is necessary. If imposter syndrome has come to visit you, congratulations: you have begun to manifest the life of your dreams. Ignore that fucker and remind yourself you are worth it. Thank it for visiting and see it to the door.

Principles for Fighting Imposter Syndrome

Here are sixteen spiritual principles I've been using to sashay away impostor syndrome when it comes to visit.

1. **Out the impostor with your journal.** Impostor syndrome often shows up as a feeling of unworthiness or doubt, or a general feeling of unease. A great way of getting clear on these feelings is to write out the negative self-talk as it comes to you and see how ridiculous it actually is.

2. **Acknowledge your various parts.** When we get swept away in anxiety, it's hard to remember that there's only a part of us that is experiencing this emotion. By conducting self-inquiry, you'll be able to tease away the part

of you that feels fake or nervous and identify other parts of you that are excited and feel capable. Anxiety is never our only experience.

3. **Know you are not alone.** Impostor syndrome is a universal experience among mega bosses. We all experience it, so welcome to the club!

4. **Collect evidence to the contrary.** Everyone has accomplished something amazing. Make a list of your accomplishments to reference so you can remind yourself that your impostor story is fabricated.

5. **Understand how you are actually perceived.** Write out a list of things you appreciate about yourself. If you're having a hard time writing this list, call a friend and say, "I'm having impostor syndrome. Can you tell me the things you appreciate about me?"

6. **Reframe doubt as positivity.** Instead of "I don't know anything," you can say, "I know enough" and "I am enough."

7. **Your feelings are real but not true.** Although your impostor syndrome may feel like a true depiction of reality, it is not. Remember that sometimes our feelings lead us to more abundance and trust, but sometimes they lead us backward.

8. **Practice daily meditation and breathwork.** When we meditate, we create space between our innate qualities and the lies that we tell ourselves. And practicing breathwork, belly breathing (chapter 4, page 91) in particular, can be helpful in creating space and slowing down racing thoughts.

9. **Don't underestimate your bravery.** When you move forward, even when you are scared, it gives everyone else permission to move forward, too. All it takes is one step.

10. **Take a tough-love approach.** I've been known to tell myself things like, "Sorry, honey, you're going to die someday anyway, so we might as well do the work. What's the worst that could happen?"

11. **You're always changing.** The fact that things are always changing is not optional; it is totally out of our control. It's which direction you're heading that you can control.

12. **Don't wait for permission.** Don't let credentials hold you back. Success is more than just a diploma.

13. **Smile.** It could make a huge difference.

14. **Look outside of yourself.** Helping others is often the best way to get out of a negative thought spiral. Help someone genuinely, and you'll feel your inner critic quiet down.

15. **Record positive interactions.** The brain is more likely to remember negative interactions than positive ones—this is our negativity bias. To counter this bias, keep a file of all the good things people have said about you. I'll take screenshots of all the nice messages and comments that have touched my heart over the years.

16. **Know that comparison is death.** Stop comparing and competing. These narratives will keep you trapped in impostor syndrome.

May You Live with Ease

When we are in the flow state—a state of ease—we are creating a life of manifestation. It's that simple. It's easier to create abundance when there's less struggle. When there's a sense of mental effortlessness, a feeling that life moves you forward. This is where the new-age cliché "go with the flow" comes from—this idea that life will guide you toward the people, places, and things that support your purpose *if* you have the attitude to match.

Until you truly believe in yourself, it takes daily rituals and habits to make this your new default. Let's try one practice now. Take a moment and repeat to yourself, "Whatever I can imagine, it is possible to become my reality." Repeat this at least seven times, up to twenty-one times.

Not only do you have to believe in yourself to manifest, what you want has to be supported by the heart. Remember heart goals vs. mind goals? Make sure what you want is from the heart and not your conditioned mind, your mom, your grandma, your sister, or society.

Here is a visualization exercise you can use morning and night to support an abundance mindset. This way we reinforce change at the neurological level and create new neural pathways. We are training the power of our imagination to visualize this new state of abundance.

Abundance Visualization

Gently settle into a comfortable position, either seated on a chair or lying down, and close your eyes.

Now ask yourself, *What does abundance mean to me?* Maybe it means lots of money, loving friends, travel, adventures, having a healthy body and a clear mind, a new home, a family, a community, work that you love . . .

Allow the answers to come to you, and release any self-judgment that arises. You're worthy of all forms of abundance!

Now, visualize yourself walking in a forest, feeling the sun coming in through the leaves. You look up to see how tall the trees are, you feel wet grass underneath your feet, you feel crisp forest air brushing by your arms and cheeks, and you continue to walk until you see a clearing. As you get closer to the clearing and enter it, I want you to see yourself surrounded by all these forms of abundance, whatever "abundance" means to you.

Visualize yourself there with these forms of abundance.

Now go up to every single person and thing there and say: *I am worthy of having you! This is my heart's wish, and I am worthy of you!*

Continue to let all forms of abundance know that you are worthy of them.

Now repeat three times: *Because I can imagine this, it's possible for this to be my reality.*

And slowly, when you're ready, open your eyes.

The Power of Intention

Our words carry weight, just as our thoughts, feelings, and emotions do. Therefore we need to be responsible with our words. We must be clear about the power of words, very clear about the fact that when we are talking, we are casting spells with our words. Each word we speak, either to ourselves or aloud, is charged with the intention you infuse it with. It's important to check yourself when you casually say absolute words like "never," "hate." It's important to remove these words from our vocabulary. They block manifesting. They are not the kind of intention you want to bring to your life. What promotes positive intention is gratitude. Having a daily gratitude practice and an accountability partner is a great way to increase the positive intention in your life. You can begin a self-practice of writing three things you're grateful for every morning, or better yet, you can make this a group activity. Try sending the three things you're grateful for to a trusted friend every morning and exchange gratitude. This way, you are creating a ripple effect of positivity not only in your life, but also in someone else's. I check in with my *sangha* (my spiritual community) on a daily basis; we exchange voice notes, because I'm constantly traveling. It is such a powerful way to share good intent as a practice.

PRACTICE, PRACTICE, PRACTICE

Sometimes you take two steps back before you take one forward. Every day is different. Every day, actually every moment, is an opportunity to stay the course, use a tool from your sassy toolkit, and keep it moving in the direction of your dreams.

On this path called life, every single day, you are going to experience moments where your values are questioned and myriad forms of obstacles. Obstacles can shapeshift. The obstacle could be your boss telling you you're not ready for a promotion, your dad's inability to say he loves you, your so-called friend being shady behind your back. It could be being rejected by a romantic partner, or facing rejection in your craft; it could be blowing an interview and not getting a job you really want; it could be waking up feeling like trash for no apparent reason or a shame spiral because you relapsed after doing so well for so long.

What all of these obstacles (life) have in common is that they require a response from you. Nothing can happen *to you* without your permission. Things happen all the time. But they happen to you when you let them in, react, and get carried away in the pain of reaction. When the obstacles of life happen, is it possible to let them happen without getting emotionally entangled? Is it possible to respond in a healthy way without letting the pain start running the show again?

Let's go over these examples and how the different responses look.

Obstacle to progress: Your manager says you're not ready for the promotion.

Shame response: I'm not good enough.

Mega boss response: This is not a reflection of my potential, only where I am now. I'm not giving up. I'm open to feedback and growth.

Obstacle to progress: Dad doesn't say "I love you."

Shame response: I'm not lovable. (Goes down rabbit hole of unlovability.)

Mega boss response: That's dad's shit to work out. Even though I'm hurt, I'm grateful I know how to show love.

Obstacle to progress: A friend looks you up and down and says, "Are you sure you want to wear that?"

Shame response: I am ugly/bad/not good enough.

Mega boss response: I feel powerful and confident. People's judgments usually have more to do with them than with me.

My goal is to give you so many different tools in so many different ways that you finally understand that you're worth it, that you finally believe in you (with intention), that you aren't set back by life anymore. I want you to be resilient when life happens because life is going to happen every single day. Your untrained mind is not going to stop trying to trick you into believing its stories, people aren't going to stop being assholes and triggering you. It's about choosing freedom. Again and again and again and again.

> ## Quick Mirror Practice
> Look at yourself in the mirror for as long as it takes to let yourself soften before your eyes. Let whatever perceived flaws you think you have soften.
> Send love to all parts of yourself.

Moment by Moment

If you are moving forward, you are setting yourself free. One of my teachers said that there are sixty-five moments in every snap of a finger. Every waking moment, we have an opportunity to be fulfilling our mission and our dreams. It's just a matter of choice, a matter of commitment, and a matter of taking small steps in the right direction. Don't worry about doing it right. Don't worry about timing. Every waking moment is an opportunity for complete enlightenment. Start with five minutes. It really comes down to a daily commitment to your freedom.

Every moment of every day has the power to get you closer to the life you want and deserve. Why? Because every day is full of choices. Do you choose to move in the direction of the You of your dreams or the you of your past? We must see each moment as a choice to choose You or to choose fear. Choose to grow or choose to stay stuck. It is truly up to you. The beauty of being human is that every day is an opportunity to grow.

So, yes, there are sixty-five opportunities in every snap of a finger, but don't be overwhelmed by that; just say, "Wow." Submit to the awe of life. Look how much potential there is in the world and in your day for you to pivot out of the shit show and into the powerful life you're here to create. Life isn't a dress rehearsal; it's time to step onto the stage now.

Awaken Your Inner Sass

Step 5: Name your superpower.

Just like your purpose and mission, your unique gifts (innate superpowers) are not going to look like anyone else's. As you've been learning, what you want to heal in the world and what you're curious about are unique to you, and how you put it all together becomes your path. But there's one more piece. Each of us has special gifts we are meant to share with the world. I am a teacher; I've found a love and gift for sharing wisdom and helping as many people as possible find their way to healing. Another one of my special-sauce superpowers is my sass. This is why the book is called *Spiritually Sassy*. It's my hard-won superpower of being totally and completely myself in all my extra-ness that I want to share with you so you may be empowered to be You in your truest sense, using all of you on your journey. My sass wasn't always something I loved about me. For a long time I was ashamed, in the closet, trying to be as small as possible in many parts of my life, but now it's something I find power in. It's so often that the thing that initially causes us the most pain is the thing, once reframed, we most need to share with the world. In this chapter we're going to find what yours is. Chances are, you probably already have a good idea, but maybe a fear of being really and deeply You has you afraid to show the world your bright colors. We're going to work through all of that. People will adjust. If it's too bright, they can wear sunglasses. It's not your problem.

BECOMING A SPIRITUAL SUPERHERO

What if we actually entered into this life with a karmic contract, and part of that contract was to figure out how to clear our mental delusions, discover our superpower, and create from it? What if that was our purpose? What if *using* your superpower, bringing your *it* to the forefront, was the purpose of this go-round here on Earth? What if you just can't remember making this karmic contract? For a moment, let's play around with the idea that you really did, and you're remembering for the first time that this is what you signed on to.

The concept for *Spiritually Sassy* came about from my early days on my spiritual path when I realized I was mimicking "ultra-spiritual" people. It's funny to look back and see it now. All of these people I was trying to emulate, they were doing the best they knew how, caught in their own mental patterns, working out their own karma and kinks, and I was putting them on a pedestal. They were my model for what a spiritual person acted, sounded, and looked like.

I was not seeing clearly. As I furthered my study, traveled, and got to see other examples of what "spiritual" could be in the world, I discovered living masters and teachers and saints in India and Nepal who were so different from the other teachers I knew. They were . . . sassy, full of life, and bold.

So, what do I mean by "spiritually sassy" as a superpower? First, I believe developing ourselves spiritually and helping others do the same is the purpose of human life.

Whatever path you decide to take, spirituality is all about realizing that the obscurations of the mind are keeping us locked away from the heart. For each of us, our path is to clean up the things that are in the way of us and our heart, our essence. "Sassy" is an invitation to live boldly, flamboyantly, high vision, full power! It doesn't end here, though: we must give these tools away. Share! This is key.

Being spiritually sassy is not only something I do for me; being spiritually sassy is also about being of benefit to others. By now you've realized that by diving deep into your own spiritual path, you are helping others to do the same. You'll do so in such an authentic, unique way, other people will realize their own unique, individual superpowers and gifts just by seeing someone living their spiritually sassy curriculum fully. What good is it to realize we have an infinite well of possibility within ourselves, lying there dormant, and not put it to use? This completely radiant rainbow light, the heart, full of courage, possibility, potential, infinite resources, first needs to be found by you, and then it should be shared with the world. What use is it to know it's there and keep it to yourself? There's no fun in that.

Being spiritually sassy means we've realized we're wired to bond, we're wired to connect, and that *through* connection, we go to the next level. The spiritually sassy path is not the ascetic path to enlightenment. The spiritually sassy path is the tantric path to enlightenment. That means it's all about utilizing everything we have within us and everything life has to offer to become free.

Name Your Power

When I talk about superpowers, I am talking about talents or gifts. These words are old paradigm, though. Let's redesign. The new paradigm is about superpowers. We have superpowers! There, I said it. The truth is, our conditioning has limited our superhuman capabilities. So, when we use words like *superpower*, it helps us remember that we do in fact have superhuman capabilities, capacities, and potential.

Superpower. Gift. Talent. There are many names for what I'm talking about. Remember when I asked you to have a conversation with your purpose? Like, "Hey purpose, what do you want me to do?" The way purpose responds is through your natural talents.

Purpose and superpowers go hand in hand in that superpowers help us live our purpose. The first sign that purpose is trying to find you is that you feel stuck. You feel like you're living the same movie over and over again, through daily routines and repetitive psychological patterns. When the repetition becomes too much and you say to yourself, "I want spontaneity, I want adventure, I want change," and you feel inspired to seek that—that is you activating your purpose and superpowers. That pull, that voice: that's purpose and your inner superhero saying, "Hey girl. Come." When our days become repetitive, we are missing the spice of life. Sometimes purpose even whispers to you in dreams.

The definition of purpose is using your superpower. The goal is that when you are in touch with your superpower, you are replenishing your internal resources, living from the heart, connected to an inner well of joy, clarity, compassion, and wisdom. Therefore your default is . . . happy. Once you begin to exercise your superpowers, you want others to have that experience, too. Everyone has the opportunity to exercise their own superpowers—their unique capabilities, capacity, and potential. Superpower combined with purpose allows you to not only do for yourself, but for the collective.

Like everything having to do with the heart, superpowers are usually hidden. We often have to dig deep inside ourselves or go through a lot of growth to tap into them, let alone have the courage to share them. But the heart is waiting for you to find it. It will be your Work to do so.

GETTING OUT OF YOUR COMFORT ZONE

Growth is beautiful once it's done and you're on the other side, but not so fun as you're experiencing it. You experience the growing pains of moving on from an old self into a new one, and they hurt. Along with the triggers and fears that may be stirred up, as well as the loneliness of trying to find where you fit in, all kinds of painful things can take place when you're growing. Everything feels uncomfortable in the process.

Imagine there are three overlapping circles: the comfort zone, the growth zone, and the overwhelming zone.

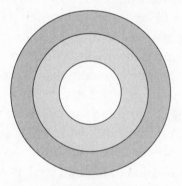

The comfort zone is the inner circle,
the circle outside the comfort zone is the growth zone,
and outside of that is the overwhelming zone.

Although growth and change are natural laws, we sometimes need to encourage them, especially when we feel stuck. It will certainly not feel joyous to step out of your comfort zone, into the growth zone, and all the way into the overwhelming zone all at once. What feels overwhelming now may be a result of your particular conditioning. We need to step out of the comfort zone into the growth zone and take just a few steps into the overwhelming zone every day in order to expand the comfort and growth zones so much that the overwhelming zone shrinks. From a psychological perspective, this is called exposure therapy. Basically, in order to move forward, we need to do small things every day that scare us in order to build courage and prepare for the life we want.

It's important to mention, as we talk about dreams and abundance and all that, that our mission in life won't be easy. Sometimes, the superpower will stem from a very painful or traumatic experience. But in that case your resilience, the beauty you've created from it, is to be your superpower, and you are meant to help others get through similar experiences. This means that because of your mission, you may often be surrounded by people who are in very challenging circumstances. I don't want you to think anyone's high-vision mission will be flowers and sunshine, all the time. No, many of us will be dredging through trauma and tough emotions; many will be holding space for others experiencing the same. I don't know what your particular mission is or what your superpower is. Only you know. Your mission may come to life from a trauma you've experienced, and your purpose may be to share the tools that have helped you transform this trauma. Don't worry that you haven't fully healed from whatever it is that happened to you; healing is ongoing. The point is that whatever has helped you get a glimpse of insight, *that* is what you need to share. Purpose doesn't look the same for everyone. We need to know that our mission will not be effortless. Sometimes the mission is quite challenging, and that's okay, too.

When you start to get clarity on what it is you are meant to do, that's when you'll know it's time to step outside of your comfort zone little by little. The idea is that the growth zone is exactly that: growth. This is where we get challenged, where we learn. The overwhelming zone is where you are really stretched. It's downright scary here because you are tested and expected to step up in ways you never have. Little by little, you can start to master this zone and get more comfortable when it presents itself.

I recently visited the overwhelming zone. I was in Nepal, and I had an opportunity to visit an ancient cave surrounded by lots of mystical lore. This cave was physically extremely dangerous to enter, and it was even more dangerous to explore, requiring Spider Man–like moves not to fall deep down and die. For me, this embodied the overwhelming zone. I *chose* to do something I was terrified of. I was *willing* to take a risk in order to grow. I knew this cave had something to offer me, and indeed, I had a mystical experience while there. It was physically dangerous, yes, but also emotionally dangerous. The deeper down I went, the more feelings started to come up. Old stuff I thought I had resolved. It all came to dance at the same time—insecurities, deep feelings of hurt and regret, imposter syndrome, self-loathing, and shame. I met all these parts of myself, one by ugly one, and I had the opportunity to uncover a new level of spacious awareness and deeper compassion to be with these feelings, let them pass, and not become them, without them leaving any psychological aftertaste. This was what the cave had to offer me. The experience is not something I could ever recreate; what's significant is that I did it when the right opportunity arose. As you continue to develop yourself, you'll know when it's time to step into the overwhelming zone and experience all the growth that's there for you. I think of it as taking a spiritual lawnmower to unwholesome karmic weeds that have started to sprout unbeknownst to you, and despite all the work you've already done. Each day is going to offer you your own version of an ancient, mystical cave in Nepal, and you will have the opportunity to go in or stay put. Are you willing to grow? Are you willing to enter?

This is not to say that you can't find your purpose in the comfort zone, but you won't be able to fully live your purpose there. That day at the cave, I had a friend who decided not to enter; that was fine, that was his choice. In that moment, he needed to stay in his comfort zone, where there was already enough growth for him. But I strongly believe that in the big picture, we need to step out of our comfort zone, into the growth zone, and then into the overwhelming zone in order to actually live our purpose.

When I say you may be able to find your purpose in your comfort zone, that's because it may be right in front of you. You just haven't looked hard enough. We need to experiment with many different things in order to go from being a dabbler to a master. How? By *doing* many different things, not all at the same time, but by giving yourself some deadlines: "I'm gonna try this out, then I'm gonna try that out." Take it step by step until the side hustle becomes the main hustle. It's in this process of trying new things, including things that scare us, that we continually get knocked down and eventually fail forward. Eventually, we bounce forward, not backward. By testing our material and regularly stepping out of our comfort zone, into the growth zone, and then into the overwhelming zone, we get to know our purpose and actually apply our gifts, our superpowers.

As you take these small steps, it's important to check in with yourself. At the end of each day, ask yourself these questions:

- What did I learn today from stepping out of the comfort zone into the growth zone?

- What did I learn today from going from the growth zone into the overwhelming zone?

- What is helping me bounce forward?

We're going to need to fall and fail multiple times as we test our material—as we follow our curiosity and activate our superpower—out in the world, not only in a holy cave in Nepal, but in your real life. When we test our material, we find what we are meant to share. It's important to remember that your superpower may be hidden by your wounds. For example, one of my wounds was that I had hurt other people and myself and had not found forgiveness. Lack of forgiveness is what led me to start learning about compassion, training my mind, traveling, and learning so much about forgiveness that it became obvious this was my path and part of my superpower as a teacher: to show people how to do the same for themselves.

I slipped on my way out of the cave and it was almost bad. Our guide grabbed me just in time, and with the tips of my fingers I struggled to catch hold of his hand. This is yet another metaphor for life. Slipping, falling, and failing are all part of the journey. There is no movement without these things, no growth. When I finally got out of the cave intact, I had such a profound sense of gratitude for life, such a pristine picture of my personal purpose, I swear, the whole universe was in on it. Dusk was approaching, and the first thing I saw as I emerged was the giant, round, full moon rising. The guide helped me out, put a gold scarf around my neck, and whispered sacred mantras in my ear. Those witnessing said there were birds flying around us in a circle. I felt like I had received a transmission for the next stage of my liberation, and I had a renewed passion to share my learnings with the world.

I'm sharing this story with you not because you need to go to Nepal and have the exact same experience (you don't!), but because this experience is such a powerful metaphor for the idea of the comfort zone/growth zone/overwhelming zone and a lesson in what can happen when you allow, when you are willing, when you go inside. Mystical experiences, spiritual transmission, and lessons from the overwhelming zone await you in the life you are in right now.

If you are in your comfort zone now, you may feel something like happiness there. That's because avoiding taking risks feels nice, it feels comfortable . . . until it doesn't, until you feel stuck or paralyzed, until your life is at a standstill. You may find temporary joy through comfort because you avoided taking a risk and can stay just a bit longer under the protection of your security blanket. Maybe you said no to something that was in the growth zone and you were happy to stay in the comfort zone, but the thing is, staying in that place doesn't lead to sustainable happiness.

We need to stop getting stuck on analysis paralysis, over-thinking, overanalyzing. Just follow the spark. If there's still a spark about something you wanted to do, stop holding yourself back. Just begin. Know that fear is the natural response to stepping out, and that soon the feeling will lessen. This is the beauty of growth.

Tapping into what really matters to you—your values—is essential for helping you pick and choose the things that are worth going out of your comfort zone for.

What Really Matters

When your values are not aligned with what you are doing, it perpetuates suffering. What matters to you? Do you know how to answer that? It will probably take you a little while to sit with that question and remember what matters most to you. The next step is to look at your life and your daily actions. What is in alignment with what you care about, and what is sending you in circles chasing things, people, places that don't really matter to you? When we don't know our values, we waste time and energy. Knowing what you value can help you make day-to-day decisions. It can even help with boundaries. You can say "no" or "yes" with intention, depending on whether that person, place, or thing aligns with your inner value system. Making choices becomes as easy as asking yourself, "Is this setting me free or keeping me stuck? Does this align with what I truly care about and where I'm going?"

Identifying your values is extremely important. I started thinking about values in a serious way back in 2014. Before that, I was humming along, working in fashion and not concerned with the language of my heart or what deeply mattered to me. What I thought mattered to me back then were fame and wealth. I didn't stop to consider that these values would not lead me to sustainable happiness, but to the opposite. I was miserable, but I was so out of touch with myself that I was numb to my own misery. It's fascinating to notice, once you start to learn about values, how out of alignment so many things are. This actually makes it easier to focus on what matters.

Your life on Earth can be so much easier when you acknowledge your values and then make plans and decisions that honor them, that support them. This is what it's all about. Values are a supportive tool to help give the life of your dreams a solid foundation. Maybe you are living as though you value making a lot of money, owning a home, and working in a corporate environment, when actually you value being in nature, building a family, and exercising your artistic abilities. So many of us are in conflict with ourselves. We've living socially acceptable lives that we don't truly want or value. When your everyday life clashes with your values, there will come a time when you just can't take it anymore, and you crash. Maybe you've already reached that point and that's why you've picked up this book.

This is what we are trying to create—preventive, holistic medicine—to support your inner values so you can create sustainable happiness. When you get clear about your values, you then get clear about how you can use them to make decisions that support a sustainable, happy life. The desire for money is a big one I often see. We chase money and it makes us crazy, but when we look inside, making a lot of money isn't what life is asking of us. Yet we spend all of our precious energy trying to get more of it, meanwhile not attending to the things that our heart wants. Hey girl, I was there for a long time. I was trapped in that money-chasing narrative, which comes from a scarcity mindset. But our true values tap into an inner richness that has nothing to do with material wealth.

A question I often ask my students is: "What is your definition of happiness?" We have been conditioned to think of happiness through someone else's unresolved traumas and unexamined belief systems, through advertising and whatever society tells us to value. We haven't taken the time to entertain that question, or even to ask it.

Just as we've been confused about mind goals vs. heart goals, so too have we been misinformed about values. Many of us have grown up thinking we value material possessions, when in reality, we come to find, after chasing those things for many years, that they don't mean much after all. "My money and good looks make me so happy," said no one ever! So, what do you really care about?

Take a moment to really reflect on that question. For fifteen minutes, free write on the following two questions.

1. What makes you happy?

2. What is your definition of happiness?

When you're done, read it back to yourself. Do your answers align? Does what makes you happy match your definition of happiness?

If you believe your purpose is about wealth and power, that's a sign you are being guided by your conditioned mind. Happiness comes from what you're doing every single day in alignment with your inner values, the small choices you're making moment to moment, not only from money or status. It's that simple. So, when you are feeling guided by those ideals, you can be sure it's a sign of an imbalance.

Living a high-vision life is aligning with our values. When you're aligned with your values, you become attracted to different things—things *you* really want, not the things society says you should have. This way, your mission and purpose, the people you need to know, the opportunities you need to receive, find you. When your mission matches your values and is aligned with the heart, you are living a high-vision life. If my values are playfulness, service, altruism, connection, community, and kindness, and every day I make an effort to get out and do things that align me with these values, then I am living a life of purpose. Every day, make an effort to water the seeds that nurture the life you want. Every day, listen to the awakened part of you. Every day, work to uncover your essence.

The beautiful, magical thing I want you to understand is that when you are living this way, you're inviting everyone you come in contact with to believe there is something special in them, too. When you live in alignment, you send a message to all those around you. This is so powerful. Sometimes making an impact is as simple as making your life an example and an inspiration to others. Have you ever been inspired to change your life, change your day, change your vibe because of someone you encountered? Trust me, you will be that for someone. You probably already are.

Clarifying Values

Circle the values you wish to cultivate. Feel free to write in any values that you don't find in this list.

manners	patience	truthfulness
kindness	consideration	health
concentration	creativity	friendship
cooperation	helpfulness	positivity
honesty	forgiveness	global stewardship
responsibility	self-acceptance	determination
generosity	loyalty	independence
self-discipline	fairness	compassion
active citizenship	perseverance	thankfulness
trust	tolerance	justice
courage	contentment	reflection
service	respect	_____
_____	_____	_____

THE ROLE OF JOY

Joy is crucial. It may seem like doing the Work is all about discipline and not fun, but that's a lie. Joy is one of the keys to living a high-vision life. A high-vision life is a life where your baseline is more joyous, more creative, and no longer based on extreme highs or lows. A high-vision life is one that accepts that we are gonna fall sometimes, but when we do, we'll fall forward. A high-vision life is a life of purpose. When we're ready to give back to the world, when we're ready to live a purposeful life, joy is right there in the process, because it is a lifelong journey. As I mentioned earlier, your mission may be a painful one, but even in that, there can be joy. Many of the steps of purification I'm leading you through in this book won't be fun, but joy is different from fun. Joy is the baseline. When you are living your values, your purpose, your mission, joy is inevitable.

Do you have a playful attitude? Can you laugh at yourself? This is how joy can be present even during hard times. Playfulness, laughter, dance, singing—these are all joyful expressions of awakening. If you're allowing yourself to be funny, to be silly, this is a means of awakening. I'm not talking about masking feelings and deflecting emotions with humor or sarcasm. I'm talking about doing the Work and letting joy emerge, letting sassiness emerge.

When we are dancing, we are in ecstasy. To me, dance is the expression of the heart shining. The new spirituality is this: it is joyful, it is raw, it is playful, it is creative, it is laughter, it is dance. This is how we bring beauty into the world. We can beautify the world with a smile, with a dance, with a laugh.

Happiness Fill-In

Finish the following sentences—they will point you toward your gift, purpose, and mission.

I feel most alive when I'm _____

Happiness feels like _____

I feel most connected when I'm _____

I feel most in alignment with my dream when I'm

_____

I feel most secure when I'm _____

I feel most alive when I'm with _____

Alignment feels like _____

I am doing what matters most to me when I'm

_____

I am connected to my life purpose when I'm

_____

I feel my best when I'm _____

Purpose feels like _____

I feel connected to my heart when I'm _____

_____

I feel most in flow when I'm _____

Flow looks like _____

When I'm in my power, I'm doing this: _____

_____

I feel most passionate when I'm _____

Passion feels like _____

When I'm sharing my gifts, I'm doing this: _____

_____

USING YOUR SUPERPOWERS

Using your gifts in this life is the most important thing. It's what you came here to do! It's top priority. As you can tell, purpose is connected and dependent on so many factors—first you must awaken enough to develop a heart connection, you must live a valued life, you must give back and share. But what is it you are to share, and how are you to share it? And is there a cost for not sharing your gifts? Yep. What if you have to come back here and do it all over again if you don't share what you have in this lifetime?

Let's look at this through the lens of love. Love is best when shown, when expressed. You can't study love. Love is not theoretical. Love is only useful when demonstrated, when put to use, for the benefit of others. The same is true for your superpowers: they must be shared in order to be fully realized. Not sharing is not moving forward. Not sharing is staying stuck, staying in the comfort zone. We're also not sharing when we're intellectualizing what we have to offer, intellectualizing spiritual growth, intellectualizing our lives instead of taking action: stepping into the unknown, learning, doing, and sharing.

Everyone has a specific set of strengths. Sometimes they're related to your wound. You overcome a wound and heal, and it's usually the process of healing that contributes to your superpower. For me, my strength has been communication. When I connect this strength to my previous wound (lack of forgiveness), it leads me to the gift of communicating compassionately and helping others heal using the tools that have helped me. Perhaps someone who overcame a dysfunctional relationship with food went on to become a holistic nutritionist. Someone who lost a parent to cancer may become a scientist focused on cancer research. Maybe someone who sought community their whole life became a café owner so they could build a community. Figure out your strength and connect it to your wound, and that will point you toward purpose. It is at that intersection where your superpower lives.

We can look at strengths another way, too. What you perceive as your weakness could actually be your strength. For example, if you have been conditioned your whole life and told you're "not good enough" in some way, then you may not have had the opportunity to nurture that part of you. You may discover that very aspect of yourself to be your greatest strength.

Earlier in this chapter you filled in the blanks for some questions related to happiness; now I want to take it one step further and focus on your superpower. Fill in the blanks below.

Superpower Fill-In

I feel wise when _____

I feel aligned when _____

I am naturally good at _____

Some consistent feedback I've received from

people closest to me is _____

I am good at _____

People tell me I'm good at _____

I feel in my element when I'm _____

I feel like I'm offering something of value when I'm

_____

I feel most natural when I'm _____

I feel most me when I'm _____

I feel I'm really helping someone when I _____

_____

I also want you to think of what you're scared of because, oftentimes, our special gift requires more work from us to discover, and this is work that requires us to courageously leave our comfort zone. Let's do one more fill-in below and see if you feel any sparks for perceived weaknesses that are begging you to find the courage to explore them.

Where My Work Is Fill-In

When I was a kid, I always struggled with _____

_____

At work, I struggle with _____

In personal relationships, I struggle with _____

_____

I've never been good at _____

When I was a kid, I was told "you'll never" or "you can't" about _____

Something I've always wanted to try but never have is _____

I wish I could _____

I admire people who _____

I want to be remembered for _____

If money was no object, I would _____

If I had the courage, I would _____

Visualizing Your High-Vision Dream

For ten to fifteen minutes, I want you to close your eyes and visualize yourself in the life you want, having made the positive changes you want to make, in an ideal situation. Feel what it is to exist in this reality. Who is with you? Where are you? What are you doing? How do you feel? Go into as much detail as possible. Guide yourself through your own dream. Take in the smells and colors and textures. Have fun with this.

Accessing Your High-Vision Self Anytime

Now write down what came up during your visualization. Focus on how it felt to be your best version of you. How do you feel now? What needs to change for you to feel the way you did in your visualization? Accessing the *feeling* of what you want is key. Once we begin to *feel* different, feel as though our lives are changing, behaviors soon follow. Much like intention, tapping into feeling is super powerful. This is your new self check-in, to be used anytime: How do I feel? If it's not the way you felt in your visualization, let that be your signal that an adjustment needs to be made. You always have access to a new state of mind.

Your One-Year Mission Statement

You now have so much knowledge about what it takes to live a life of purpose and enact your life's mission. It's time to put it all together and create your own mission statement. Every company has a mission statement. You are the CEO of you. What do you stand for? It's hard to apply this to your whole life, so let's start with the next year. What is your mission for the next year of your life? Be bold when you write your mission statement. It must motivate you and challenge your present reality. You must believe it and embrace it as your full potential. Get out a pen and paper and answer the following questions.

> **Step 1:** Get specific as fuck. What would you like to accomplish in the next year? Why? How will it help others?

Step 2: Write down the date (one year from now) on which you'll achieve your mission and circle it.

Step 3: What will you need to give up in order to accomplish your mission by this date?

Step 4: Create a plan for achieving what you desire.

Step 5: Combine your answers to steps 1–4 in a couple of sentences. For example: "I will be working as a health coach within the next year. In order to do that, I will save to pay for certification classes by cancelling my cable membership, and I will prioritize my physical and mental health every week."

Now you have your statement. Put it where you will see it in the morning when you wake up and at night before you go to bed (like on your bathroom mirror).

We can start to use our mission/goal like a mantra, sending a signal to our genes that we're safe doing this. It may feel scary, but we have to fake it till we make it. Send a signal to your whole self that working toward your goal is safe for you to do.

Working with your mission statement in this way is a practice. Act "as if": as you read it, spend some time visualizing yourself having already accomplished it, living in that world. Maybe write the mission statement down and keep it in your purse or inside your wallet. I have a student who took a screenshot and made it their wallpaper. This is now one of your tools anytime you feel wobbly or out of alignment.

REAL, BUT NOT TRUE

We all have unique circumstances in life. Maybe you were born into struggles, experienced traumas early in life or other circumstances that were especially difficult. So, let's acknowledge that for a moment. Your life circumstances are different from mine. We've all got different shit to work out, but we are all here to work it out. If you bypass it, there it always is, waiting for you. The beautiful, affirming, and egalitarian thing is, none of us possesses any secret for dealing with life. We all come in with tangled minds, and we're all here trying to figure it out together. No matter what your circumstances are, no matter who you are or where you live, you can be free.

Everybody, no matter who they are, is experiencing suffering, but there is a way out. We can all be free. I know it doesn't seem possible sometimes. *Free.* What a concept! Can you be happy? Yes! Your dreams can come true no matter who you are, no matter where you come from, no matter whether you are thirty days or thirty years from reaching your goal. You can get there. A resounding YES to all of your doubts. The answer is *yes*.

The way we think about our potential is defined by our conditioning, which is limited and limiting. We have to remember that unprocessed trauma and our neurotic habits put blinders over our eyes. Where you've been and what you've been through do not define you. Your current circumstances don't define you, either. You can choose to take a step forward every single day. This is freedom. You can acknowledge that where you are is not where you would ultimately like to be and take a baby step forward every day, and that is freedom. "I'm aware this situation is shitty, but I'm not gonna add any more shit to the shit story. I am choosing to move forward." Start where you are.

For anyone experiencing rejection regularly for being who you are, remember this: people inflict suffering onto others because they are suffering themselves. Of course, this doesn't take away from the reality that this person cursed at you or was violent with you or caused you emotional pain, but it gives you personal responsibility to continue to move forward. You can choose to move forward and forgive this motherfucker, as hard as that may be.

You hold the power. Your ability to forgive and move on is what will set you free. This is not passive! Rather, this is a powerful act of personal power and freedom.

If you have a human body, you can be free. We have to remember this when we get hooked by narratives that pull us away from our potential. Yes, love: external circumstances do not dictate your potential. We go around thinking that our circumstances are the true indicators of the quality of our internal landscape, but it's the other way around. Yes, your external circumstances can impede; sure, they can hold you back in real, frustrating ways. We can acknowledge that while our circumstances are objectively real, they are not *true*. If you're surrounded by addicts or negative people or gossip, or you live in poverty, these are real fucking limitations. "I have real limitations!" you say. Yes, they are real, they are your current experience, but they're not *true* because they're not permanent and they don't define who you are.

Our perceptions of our own circumstances are filtered and conditioned by unresolved trauma, both our own and that of previous generations. That's heavy. If you're dealing with what you perceive as external limitations—maybe you have a job that doesn't pay enough to allow you to save toward your goal or to take a class, maybe you want to go into business for yourself but are trapped in a corporate job and living paycheck to paycheck, maybe therapy and self-help are luxuries you feel you cannot afford—all of these are real, but they're not true. When we try to invest them with the truth they don't innately have, we just sound like we're making excuses.

We have to get really real, and doing this might feel like tough love. I can't tell you how often I hear people say things like, "I can't eat healthy, it's too expensive" and "I don't have time to meditate." People come up with the most creative excuses! Ask yourself: Do you want to live the same movie seventy-five years in a row? Do you want to keep living like life is a dress rehearsal? Do you want to keep feeling like shit? Do you want to allow your external circumstances to dictate the quality of your internal landscape? Or do you want your internal landscape to shape your external life? Do you want to be free? How badly do you want to be free?

Circumstances are only as real as the thickness of our conditioning. The more we chip away at that conditioning, through practices like the ones found throughout this book, the more we dissolve our convoluted and cluttered perception about what is real and true about us, and the more we see potential everywhere. The more we see the light coming through the brokenness. The more we understand that we can pull things together and be resourceful in even the most difficult circumstances.

Often the most resourceful people are the ones who have nothing. It is a matter of knowing that whatever you're experiencing right now absolutely doesn't dictate the quality of your life. It doesn't even have to dictate the quality of your day. Or week, or month, or year. We tend to think that what's right in front of us and the life we're living right now are the true indicators of what the rest of our life will be like. But we are forgetting a natural law of the universe: nothing is permanent. The most important thing you can do is work on your internal freedom. That is the one thing that's entirely in your control.

YOU ARE NOT FOR EVERYONE

As you work through the steps in this book, you will inevitably grow, and that will inevitably make some people in your life uncomfortable. Watching people find happiness while you stay stuck is never fun, so I want to prepare you for this reality. It is perfectly okay to part ways with someone who isn't into you living your best life.

People who are freaked out by you living your truth probably weren't among the people you envisioned in your dream. It's true that the more aligned you become, the more aligned your relationships become. Some people that used to fit, won't anymore. And new, more high-vision people will become more relevant. This is good. It is part of growth. And just as you are not for everyone, everyone is not for you. Some people, just like things and behaviors, are going to start to fall aside to make room for a sassier life.

Maybe it's time to leave a certain situation or a certain group or community. It's up to you what "leaving" means. Maybe it's energetic, like taking a break from a particular social scene or unfollowing certain people on social media. Maybe it's an actual, physical move. Maybe it means changing jobs, or establishing stronger boundaries in your life. Whatever it is, it's up to you to support the life you're building, especially as you continue to grow mentally stronger. You know it's time to leave when the people around you are completely stuck. Work with the life you have, and start small—small breaks can be hugely powerful. When you've rebuilt and replenished your inner resources, then you can come back and test your material.

One thing I guarantee, honey, is that when you're living your spiritually sassy path, you will become a catalyst for others' awakening—you will inspire people, make people who aren't ready to change jealous, and trigger people to see their own stuff. But don't you get taken by that. When you stop being a matchbox and become the flame, people will not know what to do with you. You, with your full rainbow-ness and sassiness, loving and believing in yourself. You best believe this will be triggering for people who are still stuck. Don't take it personally. Let them see that your sassiness is an invitation for them to be sassy, too.

The path may be lonely for a while, but rest assured, your life will recalibrate around the new you. If you go on hiding your gifts, you will be even more alone. Stop hiding your magic. Stop hiding your sassiness. Your tribe will eventually find you. It is through your sassiness, through your magic, your rainbow-ness and boldness, that we can see each other, that we can find each other.

Early on in my journey, I would get so excited about what I was learning, and I'd think everyone around me was ready for the kinds of commitments and vows and transformation that I was making. But many people were not ready. Most people we'll encounter on our path do not fully know their heart; they may be so trapped in internal chaos that they can't begin to meet you in the new place you're in. Their work is not yours to do for them. It's your job to nurture yourself and know that as you are looking for your tribe, your tribe is looking for you, too. The more you work on yourself, the more you are creating the conditions for your external life to match who you are inside.

You'll see that moments of complete connection will happen more and more. You will begin to have glimpses of something that's much bigger and more powerful than can be described with language.

Once you say, "Bye, girl," to your past life, it's not as if parts of it are not going to come find you. That's not how it is. Remember, we have been poisoning ourselves through our mind, body, and speech for years. For years we've been shackling ourselves and hiding ourselves from our spiritual heart, so it's not as easy as, "I'm moving, I'm leaving, I'm changing jobs, I'm getting out of this relationship, I'm saying goodbye to my old life, I'm leaving everyone behind." That's nice, but as I said, you've nurtured those seeds for a long time, so they will continue to bloom every once in a while.

While we can't ever completely wipe out the past and our old thought patterns, we can redesign our relationship to them. Something shitty happens, and my response?: "What is the lesson here?" Lessons and blessings, honey. That's all life is. We get better at falling and getting right back the fuck up again. You may have broken a heel, but guess what? You got duct tape in your bag! You tape that shit up and keep moving. Rise up. Work, work, work. Serve. Serve the looks, honey. This is all you got.

It's not that you just start the spiritual path and everything goes away. We have a lot of work to do, and the old seeds will continue to bloom. When they do, we choose. It's always a choice, honey. We must constantly make choices, moment by moment.

Overcome the Fear of Being Amazing

Step 6: Believe you're amazing.

You already know the recipe—now it's time to cook! It should be easy, right? Well, we know that's not true. We know it takes moment-by-moment awareness and skillful decision-making. Also, we can only succeed if we *believe* we can. We've discussed negative self-talk and limiting self-beliefs, but there are other, lingering fears that will creep up when you start to make progress. The fear of success, the fear of making money, the fear of not being enough, the fear of shining—these will blossom as you go along, and you'll need tools for understanding them. Self-doubt, insecurity, and social comparison are the killers of dreams and a recipe for inaction. We did all this work, friend. We rewrote the story of your life and identified your mission and dream. You visualized yourself living it. Now, what's in the way? Oftentimes, it is our fear of actually succeeding at what we set out to do that is the most stubborn barrier to achieving our goals. This fear may be very old and can manifest in sneaky ways. It may be the inclination to turn down an opportunity or to set your pay rate too low out of fear of abundance. It may manifest as feelings of jealousy at someone else for shining, or it could feel like paralysis to take action. In this chapter, we'll explore all of these manifestations of fear, and I'll give you tools for keepin' it moving in the direction of your goals and dreams.

THE WORLD NEEDS YOU TO SHINE

"You're too much!" "You're crazy!" "You're wild!" "You're extra." You're too too too too too. Guess what? It is time to say fuck off to all these stories because this is what it will take for you to stop being afraid of being amazing.

When you show up bright, you're lighting up the way for other people. Do you think your bright light is only lighting your way? No, honey. Your amazing-ness, your boldness, your extra-ness, your sassiness is not only helping you, boo boo! It is lighting up the bridge for us all.

We all go through ebbs and flows where we're in the light and then in the dark. But sometimes, we're more in the light than the dark because we've already been doing the work. We get to reap the harvest of our virtuous efforts and be in the world testing our material.

The more you are in the light, the more you are in your heart. The more you are in your amazing-ness, your extra-ness, the more you are in your brightness. And we need you, bright being, to keep lighting the way! We need you because so many people are so deeply rooted in the darkness. I'm not saying "darkness" in the sense of evil. I mean darkness as confusion and delusion. We depend on people who reside in the heart, in tune with the power of the heart and rooted in their true essence, who are awake and extra enough to be bold and bright for the rest of us. It's true that your path will look different from someone else's, but imagine we are all in the forest looking for the same clearing. There will be many ways to get to there. You lighting the way for yourself, lights the way for others.

All paths lead to the clearing. All paths lead to complete awakening and freedom. But we need you to be bright, okay? It's kind of like living in the growth zone and over-whelming zone more of the time. Little leftover blooms of conditioning will pop up in your mind, and you may doubt what you're doing, being so bright.

FEAR, THE GREAT TEACHER

When you are focused on a vision and see a clear path, here comes fear, trying to keep you safe. The part of the brain where fear breeds is the reptilian brain; it truly thinks shit is trying to kill you in a jungle, so, even on an average day, when your life is not at all at risk, it sends fear signals throughout your body. The brain hasn't caught up with evolution—the brain is trying to keep you alive and pro-tected from danger, from, you know, lions and tigers and shit.

Similarly, when you are trying to do great things, but great things that scare you a little, fear comes in like, "Are you sure?!" "Is it safe?!" In this case, as in the case of anxi-ety, fear is simply a signal that the status quo is being questioned and your system is freaking out. "But change is scary! We could lose everything! We might fail!" Fear is screaming all this shit in the background while you are trying to make progress, and if you don't have the wisdom to know the difference between a real lion and a lion your mind has created, you could make a decision based in fear instead of move in the direction of your dream. Thank your fear for letting you know what's important to you. Notice how, when you really care about something, fear shows up. Try noticing when that happens and quietly thank it for the information.

Imagine that when fear arises, you don't fight it. Instead you say to it, "Wassup bitch, wanna dance?" You know this game, and you're not falling for it; you're in control. You won't be scared of fear anymore. Instead, fear simply becomes an indicator that you're upleveling. Fear is letting you know you're a mega boss who isn't afraid to step out of the comfort zone. Fear is a way for you to know, "Okay honey. Welcome to the spiritually sassy club of mega bosses." Because if fear's not knocking on your door as you move through the exercises and become brighter and brighter and do more work, then you're too deep in the comfort zone. Shit's gonna come up. If it's not, then you're not doing it right.

Fear may show up as imposter syndrome, the fear of being a fraud and the feeling that you don't belong or deserve to be where you are. This is something we all experience. I'll share an experience I had. I met one of my spiritual teachers in Nepal on my twenty-seventh birthday. In the midst of a thirty-day meditation retreat, I was one of five attendees granted the honor of meeting this Lama. As I sat in his waiting chamber, my excitement was buried under overwhelming sensations of fear and self-doubt. All I could think about was how he would see me as a fraud. How I wasn't worthy of his attention. How he would sense my brokenness and send me off. I met with him three more times in the coming week, with thoughts of unworthiness each time. But in the end, everything ended up being just fine—better than fine, actually. That was fear arising, simply alerting me that I had left my comfort zone.

I wish I could say this moment of unworthiness was an isolated incident, spurred by the overwhelming experience of meeting a spiritual leader. But through so many big opportunities in my life, feelings of awe and gratitude have been buried by a massive, steaming pile of self-criticism. Instead of enjoying the ride, my mind instantly lists all the evidence it can muster to show I'm not good enough. And if the mind can't find any evidence, it makes it up! Does this sound familiar?

We need to continuously out the fear, like, "Bitch, I see you. I'm fine." Hush it and tell it you're okay. There is no lion. And go about your business. We need to remember that when fear shows up, when insecurity shows up, it feels like a true depiction of reality, but it is not. Some of our thoughts and feelings lead us to more abundance and trust, but more often, unless we've done the work, they will lead us backward.

Fear is never your entire experience. It's only ever just one part of you that is experiencing fear. *You* are not fear. You are not afraid. It's nothing more than an old karmic seed in bloom, a lesson, that's asking you to notice it and weed it out. No need to let it take over your entire experience. Go into the garden, uproot that shit. Leave. Don't spend too much time there.

Every time I overcome some fearful karmic bloom, I make a point to wish this for all beings. It's a powerful practice that helps me remember it's not all about me. Every time you are able to overcome a fear and get to the next level, try making an offering to all beings: "May all beings who are experiencing fear reconnect with their inner wisdom and inner strength." Whenever possible, don't let it be all about you. As you continue to uplevel and overcome the remaining blocks in your mind, try wishing the same for all beings. "I wish for all beings to overcome_____." Abundance lives in this offering, this generosity is a natural inclination. Wishing others well reconnects you to the natural law of abundance in a beautiful way.

OVERCOME THE FEAR OF BEING AMAZING

Doubts, insecurities, fear, shame, low self-esteem, low self-worth—all of these might return and try to convince you against the direction you're going and set you back. And a lot of internal struggle will come up as you start to overcome your fear of being amazing. But we can start to recognize some of the patterns of the mind so we can stop them in their tracks before they pull us out of the present moment and spiral us back into old ways of feeling.

Nagarjuna, an Indian Buddhist philosopher in the second century CE, identified eight specific mind patterns that we must watch out for as we start to overcome the fear of being amazing. These are referred to as the the eight worldly concerns. According to these 8 worldly concerns, we are trapped in this vicious cycle seeking to fulfill four of them—happiness, praise, fame, and gain—and doing everything in our power to run away from the other four –suffering, insignificance, blame, and loss. Unless we develop a secure enough connection with our awakened heart and the tools to know better, we will continue to stay trapped battling with ourselves, our lives and the people in it, holding close everything we like and running away from anything we don't. Getting swept up in any of these extremes can unknowingly water seeds of confusion in the karmic garden of our mind. Learning to identify how these eight patterns and tendencies can show up in your life can act as reminders to help you pay attention to when you might be caught up and be unknowingly nurturing harmful seeds in your own life and block amazingness. Notice them, acknowledge them, and then reaffirm and return to your heart.

1 & 2: Happiness vs. Suffering

As you start to make progress and recognize your innate amazingness, the next step to uncovering more of your true essence is to let go of unintentionally running around like a thirsty animal that is never satisfied. Catch yourself when you start to believe your happiness is dependent on your senses constantly being fed with only pleasant experiences. "I need to hear nice things!" "I need to taste nice things!" "I need to touch nice things!" "I need to smell nice things!" "I need to see nice things!" "I need to feel nice!" If you are constantly craving and chasing the quick pleasure that comes from the senses you will never be satisfied. This is a classic form of suffering. When we constantly chase good feeling after good feeling, we never build a muscle for coping with the unpleasantness of life. But unpleasantness is a natural part of life—grief, pain, despair, sadness—that requires us to meet it with awareness, not by running away. You will experience unpleasant sensations, and that is OK, in fact it is necessary. As a spiritually sassy warrior, you become empowered by your hardships. Your genuine happiness and your amazingness shines from your awakened heart and is not dependent on external factors. When you catch yourself chasing sense gratification, remind yourself that genuine happiness does not come from the outside, a quick way to exercise your amazingness is by wishing that all people be free of insatiable cravings.

3 & 4: Fame vs. Insignificance

In the age of social media especially, we live in a fame-obsessed culture. We all want to be special, and what lies beneath that desire is the fear of being insignificant. You have to matter to *you*. Turn to one of your mantras and remind yourself daily that you matter, you're worthy, you're deserving of the earth. You are doing this for your own personal freedom, not for fame.

5 & 6: Praise vs. Blame

How much of what you're doing is for the praise and approval of others? How much of what you do in life is for you? Do you chase validation? Are you addicted to praise? And honey, check yourself when you start to blame the world for not receiving the praise you think you deserve. No more yo-yo! When you find yourself depending on praise and unable to lift yourself up, or in a blame spiral, remember that your actions are not for validation, but for your awakening. Turn to a mantra to remind yourself that you believe in you, or take a few deep breaths and connect to the part of you that never stops believing in you. Approve of your damn self!

7 & 8: Gain vs. Loss

We have cultural norms that have been put in place by people who are deeply suffering and far from their sassy heart. We have learned to believe that more is better, that having a bigger house is better, that the more you accumulate the happier you will be. Getting things when you want has become the synonyms of a happy life, and when you don't get what you want or you lose what you have, you feel miserable, you believe that your worth is dependent on what you have to show for. Simplify your life, cultivate your best qualities of compassion, altruism, and generosity. Donate what you don't need. The more unnecessary stuff you have, the further you are from genuine connection with others and with your heart.

Mantras for Self-Belief

Self-belief requires courage. Use any of the mantras below, or recite them all when fear creeps up as you uplevel.

I have the courage to ask for what I want.

I have the courage to speak my dreams into reality.

I have the courage to be fearless.

I have the courage to step fully into my transformation.

I have the courage to let go of people and things in my life that don't support my healing.

I have the courage to love myself so deeply that it inspires others to love themselves, too.

I have the courage to be a new version of myself each day.

I have the courage to let go of my past.

I have the courage to be free.

Are You Afraid of Succeeding?

Your mind isn't exactly lying to you when it sends fear signals. Achieving your goals and dreams usually means giving up one way of life for another—giving up the status quo for something better—and change can feel scary. Let's explore what exactly you'll be giving up and obtaining with a quick cost/benefit analysis.

Reflect on these questions or feel free to write down your answers on a separate piece of paper.

If I achieve my dream, what will I have to give up?

If I achieve my dream, what will I lose? (This is the cost of your dream.)

Now reflect on these questions:

What will happen if I *don't* achieve my dream?

What will I obtain when I achieve my dream?

Will what I obtain outweigh the cost?

It is a full-time job to be your own cheerleader, to constantly remind yourself you are deserving of health, wellness, and happiness. On the road to your heart, little tricksters will constantly pop up. Self-sabotage is one such trickster. The first time I was in Nepal, after my first thirty-day retreat I left the monastery and got blackout drunk, got lost in the streets of Kathmandu, and miraculously didn't get robbed or hurt. Self-sabotage was part of my process for a while. I'd take one step forward, ten steps back. But the steps back are part of the journey forward. They contain precious learnings, so we must not judge ourselves. The saboteur comes in when you are moving forward, accomplishing your goals. It convinces you to sink back into an old pattern and fuck it up. We beat the saboteur by failing well: falling, dusting ourselves off, forgiving ourselves, and not allowing a minor setback to become a full-blown incident. You can choose to see it as a lesson and an opportunity to practice self-forgiveness.

The Comparison Game

In Buddhist psychology, comparing and competing are major causes of suffering because they are rooted in the three mental poisons. These are deeply conditioned in all minds: greed, hate, and ignorance. Out of these poisons, the top source of suffering is ignorance. It's so ignorant of us to see someone else thriving and be envious or jealous of their success instead of inspired by it. It is also ignorant to think we can have something that someone else has. We are all our own unique people on our own paths. We all bring something different. We suffer because we're looking at the success of others through the lens of ignorance. Delusion has turned inspiration into jealousy.

What if you took this beyond yourself—since we're all interconnected and interdependent, what if someone else's success was paving the way for you to walk a similar road? What if you saw someone with something you really want, and you were inspired by their success instead of envious of it? Someone else's success is an invitation for you to be successful.

Recognize when jealousy and envy are arising and take ownership of them. Nobody else is making you jealous—*you're* making you jealous. Let go of the feelings and see if you can make this recognition a habit. As part of the habit, try wishing yourself well by saying, *May I be happy.*

Gratitude is also a great antidote for jealousy. The heart of jealousy is believing you're not good enough and that what you have is inadequate. When these difficult feelings arise, counter them with gratitude. Write down or say aloud three things you are grateful for. Send some love your way for all you have accomplished and all you have in your life. Generate compassion for yourself and send love to whomever it was you were jealous of. Wish them well as you have wished yourself well: *May you be happy.* It is hard to develop this habit, but it will be transformative to shift this negative and ignorant way of thinking about the accomplishments of others.

OVERCOMING SCARCITY MINDSET

Let's get one thing straight. You deserve success. Just like you deserve happiness. *Success* is not a dirty word. *Money* is not a dirty word. They are simply tools to get shit done, live free, and share with others. We have to stop thinking of these as dirty words. You need to love success and you need to love money. I don't mean start spending money you don't have or start climbing the corporate ladder. I mean that we have to change their emotional charge by learning to relate to them differently.

Many of us are afraid of success and money because we've never had them or we don't believe we deserve them. We give them too much power because we are afraid to lose them. We must strip them of this power and relate to them instead with an energetic charge of abundance, ease, flow, utility. Money is simply something to be used and exchanged for things in life that help us along our path. Money comes and goes, success comes and goes, so there is no need to attach all this heaviness to either. Money never did anything to you! Stop acting like it's something to fear and treat it instead like it's something you absolutely can and deserve to have.

When we talk about scarcity mindset, we think it only has to do with money, but it's about so much more than that. It's possible to have a scarcity mindset around all kinds of things: time, relationships, health, intelligence, judgment, and willpower, just for starters. Think about whether you approach any of these areas of life with a belief that it is a limited resource. Scarcity mindset is just that: a mindset. It's based on beliefs. There's no solidness to it, no permanence. It's just a concept that has conditioned us. The beauty of a mindset? It can change. What we want to do is bring in an abundance mindset and make that our habit.

Scarcity Mindset Checklist

- ☐ You believe that situations are permanent.
- ☐ Your vocabulary includes a lot of "I can't do this," "I don't have enough money," "I'm not smart enough," "I don't have enough time."
- ☐ You are very envious of others.
- ☐ You tend not to be generous (don't like to give tips, share, or donate).
- ☐ You tend to hoard what you have and have a hard time letting go of things.
- ☐ You're very critical or quick to blame others.
- ☐ You're prone to gossip.
- ☐ You secretly hope others will fail.
- ☐ You're scared shitless of change.

Abundance Mindset Checklist

- ☐ You compliment others often.
- ☐ It's easy for you to forgive.
- ☐ You want others to succeed.
- ☐ You show gratitude.
- ☐ You have access to creativity and a vast imagination.
- ☐ You enjoy sharing.
- ☐ You embrace change.

Scarcity mindset makes you feel like you don't belong, like you're always alone, like there's not enough water, food, money, or opportunities. It can be very insidious, creeping into every aspect of your life and blocking abundance. Scarcity mindset is fear on autopilot mode.

In contrast, abundance mindset is:

I always have a choice.

I am grateful.

I am aware of possibility.

I focus on what is working.

I count my blessings.

Healing Scarcity Meditation

Visualize the shackles and chains that may be tied to your heart.

Imagine yourself breaking free.

Use the power of imagination to really go there. Concentrate on the practice. If your mind wanders, that's cool—just bring it back, and gather all its energy in this powerful visualization. Keep coming back, and if resistance arises, notice that, too, and come back, again and again.

Repeat this mantra as you continue to visualize:

Dear Heart,
Help me awaken from scarcity into abundance.

Cultivating an Abundant Life

We need to be working on an abundance mindset in every area of our life. We have to shift our thinking from this nutty belief that we need to be millionaires and instead focus on being content with having enough. What are you doing every day to create a prosperous mindset?

The definition of abundance is the belief that you have enough to be able to share. Let's break this down even more. Sustainable happiness requires that you have abundant flow in the following key areas.

Abundance of Education

This doesn't mean you're constantly going after new titles or training. It simply means that you're constantly learning.

Abundance of Health

This means your body is energized with a balanced amount of physical activity.

Abundance in the Home

Does your home look and feel abundant? I don't mean with flashy furniture. But is it clean and open?

Abundance in Relationships

This does not mean having rich friends. It means your relationships are rich in connection, belonging, love, and generosity, and that you feel seen and heard.

Abundance of Spirituality

Do you practice reconnecting with your heart regularly?

Abundance in Career and Finances

An abundant career is one in which you are not only benefiting yourself, you're also benefiting others. This leads to abundant finances.

When we struggle with self-worth, either consciously or unconsciously, the mind is stuck in scarcity mindset, and the dysfunctional way we relate to money leaks into other areas of our life. Where is scarcity leaking into your life? Look at all the areas of life listed above. Where are you abundant, and where is scarcity showing up? Everything we do in one area leaks into another. Everything is connected. Maybe in some areas you're doing great, while others need your attention.

Abundance Affirmation

I am free from everything that ever made prosperity feel or seem unavailable or inaccessible to me.

Financial abundance comes to me like a magnet, drawn to me by bonds that cannot be broken.

Everything I do services the creation of abundance in my life.

Making money is as easy and natural to me as breathing.

I welcome wealth, in any form it takes.

I am skilled at managing money, and it multiplies for me in return.

I am deserving of abundant wealth.

The more I serve the world and share my talents, the more money I generate.

I am happy to help others achieve wealth beyond their wildest dreams because I trust there is an endless supply and more than enough for everyone.

Financial freedom is a reality that I deserve.

I am unafraid to share my wealth in the service of others. The more I give, the more I receive.

My financial abundance supports me to make a difference in the lives of many people.

I have endless gratitude for all I have been given and know more is yet to come.

HEALING YOUR RELATIONSHIP TO MONEY

I'm going to say it again because I want you to get comfortable with this idea and this language that is so dirty for some of us: you must also love money. You need to understand that money is energy, and we need energy to create what we need to create.

I used to have a terrible relationship with money. Not only did I think I was undeserving of it, but I also wasn't educated about it—how to save it, how to improve my credit, how to prepare my taxes. I didn't know any of that. All of that ignorance compounded the shame I felt around money. Eventually, I hired an accountant, whom I have no problem paying to do something I have no idea how to do.

This is the problem, too: we don't ask for help and we are certainly afraid to pay for it, so we try to DIY things we know nothing about. That, too, is fear of money and a sign that your grip may be too tight. Money is one of the things many people have so much baggage around, so they don't ask for help and don't even want to say the dirty word.

Abundance can absolutely be blocked by the belief that you don't deserve it. This belief may be unconscious, so you may not be aware of it or the power it has over you. Another popular money belief: that being rich is bad and being poor is noble. We must redesign this. You may feel guilty, conflicted, and out of integrity about your wish to have more money and be prosperous. You may blame your parents for not having enough money and for not teaching you how to relate to money in a healthy way. We think that having prosperity is only for a select few, not for everyone.

Or maybe you have none of these limiting beliefs, and you just don't know where to start in making more money so you choose to stay stuck and not seek out help. Maybe you have a lot of money, or perhaps you come from money and you're ashamed and feel guilt about that, too. One huge problem is that we spend a lot of time talking about the things that are going wrong and not enough time in gratitude for what is working. We focus too much on the negative. It is that simple. If we focus on gratitude, it drops us into the heart and helps us become a magnet for money.

I want to share a quick story with you that exemplifies some of the things we're discussing. I ran into a very successful friend recently in line to get into a party in Bali. The party was $25 to get in, but this friend, although very wealthy, has a scarcity approach to life, a sneaky, greedy tendency, and he wanted to get in for free. If you're the one who's always looking to get a discount, always trying to sneak in, get something for free, steal, this is scarcity mindset at work. This behavior is watering the seeds of greed in your karmic garden, and those seeds will blossom as fear of spending money. It is through being generous to others that we ourselves become prosperous. This is a natural law, as natural as the law of gravity.

I know how hard it can be, living in a world where we're conditioned by every single aspect of our lives to seek out success defined by money and prestige. So, when it comes to using money to achieve our goals, like paying for school, business supplies, an accountant, training, and certification, we're constantly like, "How can I spend time doing this if it's not going to make me any money right away?" It comes back to values and approaching all you do with an abundance mindset. Otherwise, we're trapped in this rat race and a vicious reactivity circus. Return to your values and your mission. Shut out the noise and listen to your inner compass, your inner guidance.

I'm not here to tell you about how to save for your retirement or become financially free. This is not the kind of abundance I'm talking about. I know nothing of this. It's not part of my vocabulary. Do you think I'm gonna retire? Ha. I will be teaching and dancing until my last breath. I'm talking about living *now*. Live a better life today. Get one moment of clarity and then build up to another and another. This is living. Living with abundance is all in how you think and relate to the things you want. Share, be grateful, remember that not one thing is permanent. Remember, you are worthy.

You Are Always Worth It

Everything we think, say, and do carries energy. I want to give you some ways to turn up your worth in your everyday communication. For example, having boundaries is one of the most powerful ways to send a message of worth. Saying "no" when you are making values-driven choices, or when honoring yourself in some way, conveys an energetic message. It says, "this person values themself." It changes the way others interact with you going forward.

Another powerful way to send a message is by asserting yourself. When you stand up for yourself, you show others how to treat you. You may be struggling with a tendency to accept less than you're worth in terms of payment for your work or in relationships. When you can set your rate at what you deserve and tell someone what you won't stand for in a relationship, this, too, sends a message. You're saying "no" to being treated less than and "yes" to being treated like you're worth it. Everything is a choice, and these everyday choices impact your relationship with abundance—and create the next version of You!

Other ways to send a message of worthiness to yourself and others:

- Make others feel like they're worth it (volunteer, give, share, give compliments).

- Try a power pose: Stand and walk with your chest out, shoulders back, leading with the heart. Notice your posture. We send signals with our bodies. Enter the room with power. Stand tall with power and confidence.

- Dance or practice any movement with intention. Put on a song that makes you feel sexy. Use this movement practice to connect with worthiness by embodying it!

- Go upside down. Seriously. Do a handstand or lay yourself over your couch. Somehow get yourself upside down. This is a great way to shift your perspective when you're feeling hooked and literally turn the shit around, whatever it is.

Make Peace with Ambition

There is a myth in the spiritual community that wanting nothing is synonymous with being spiritual. Girl, you have permission to wish in all forms. Wishes are the language of the heart—they're how we hear her. Wishes are how our dreams and goals and purpose speak to us. How could that be wrong? It's all about how you relate to what you deeply want. Your relationship with your deepest wishes should be rooted in love, not anxiety. Check in with your intentions. If your intentions are rooted in altruistic motives, then embrace every wish with joy. Joy is the expression of our deepest desires manifesting. How beautiful.

It's bullshit that spiritual people can't be ambitious. In the modern world, ambition is necessary for many of us. But first we need to ask: What is ambition? What is success? If our ambition is completely rooted in chasing money and prestige because we believe they'll lead to happiness, then our ambition is false. We are bound to find suffering in the end. If our ambition is driven by external validation, praise, and everyone telling us how great we are, then we're fucked. This is mind ambition. But ambition with purposeful intention is healthy. This is ambition that stems from the heart.

Mind ambition is unsustainable. It is rooted in selfish motives. Heart ambition is sustainable and is rooted in altruistic motives. For example, you may be driven to get success and wealth, but your motive is to help as many people as possible. This kind of ambition is rooted in compassion. You do things because you wish for other people to be happy and free of suffering. How epic that these are your ambitions! This is the playground for abundance and prosperity, success and power, wisdom and joy. If your ambition is based on giving back, nothing and no one can take away what you came here to do!

Joyous Ambition

Are you joyful about what you want, or stressed about it? When we're joyful about our dreams, we've integrated them into the heart. They are no longer mixing with the fear of the conditioned mind. They have gotten deeper into our being, from head to heart, and we can feel the difference. You move from *I think* to *I am*. You become the joyous expression of your dream rather than the anxious and fear-ridden whisper that your dream used to be. Have fun! Laugh! Be with your dream. Let it beam from you! Let the joy of it take you. This is what being aligned with heart looks and feels like.

LIKE ATTRACTS LIKE

Finding flow and cultivating abundance in your life has a trickle-down effect. As you become more aligned with your dream and start emanating joy in your everyday interactions, watch how you begin to attract what you need: people; opportunities; new, like-minded friends. The law of abundance works both ways. People will find you, but also, you will find yourself becoming attracted to people who are out there doing what you want to be doing. Follow this. Let yourself be inspired by people. If jealousy is anxiety and scarcity in action, inspiration is the action of the heart and a sign that you've cleared out self-doubt, that you've made peace with your dream, and that it emanates from you.

Let's go back for a moment to this idea of coming into this world with contracts. I like to think about attraction like this: we are constantly finding the tools and learning the skills we need to be able to graduate from the contracts we came in with. Each time we graduate, we enter a new contract. We are constantly attracting the opportunities we need to improve our connection to the heart and develop its qualities. These come in the form of lessons and blessings. We attract what we need to learn for the phase of life we are currently in. Every opportunity that shows up (good or bad), we have attracted it so we can learn what it has to teach about how to move through the current contract. You become aware of what you need to learn and grow once you start to do the work. Each time you graduate, you are setting yourself free.

Living in Your Full Power

Step 7: Use what you have.

My friend, you have learned to speak to yourself with love. Now it is time to extend that compassion to all you do. You are the messenger and the embodiment of the beautiful mission you were sent to joyfully accomplish. If your work is only about you, it is incomplete. The Work starts with us and extends outward, into all we do, all we touch, just as self-compassion becomes compassion for others. The universe you create around you is a reflection of who you are inside.

We've done a lot of internal work in the previous chapters; now let's look outside and see what we have manifested and how we can set up our external world, too, in a way that supports our well-being and health.

LIFE, THE GREATEST TEACHER

By now you've realized that, having a human body and human experience, if you're not continuously doing the Work, your life will play on repeat. You realize that the people and things you encounter are opportunities for growth. You realize that you can heal.

By now you've also realized that all of the ways we see life from a place of lack, all of the ways we see ourselves as undeserving, unworthy, inadequate—these are all contracts/curriculums that we came here to work out. If you think about it from this perspective, it's kind of fun. You graduate from a curriculum and then you get to start a new one. Life is an adventure of growth!

On this adventure, doing this work, it's important to have a team in place. We talked about this before. Your community is evolving. Your network may have changed. It's important to know who you can call if you relapse, who your cheerleader is when you don't believe in yourself. You should also be thinking about what you have to offer your circle in the same way. The Buddha said to one of his most accomplished students, "Ananda, the sangha is the whole path."

Remember the cave story I shared with you earlier? Well, guess who was there with me in that moment? My friends. In order to grow, we need people. We need each other. That day, going deep into that cave and allowing what ended up being a transformative spiritual and emotional experience for me, I was empowered to make the choice I did because of the strength and support of my friends. Nothing happens in a vacuum, friends. In a sense, we are never truly alone and never truly independent.

IT'S YOUR PARTY . . . WHO'S INVITED?

Friendships, as loving as they are, can be attachments as well. Say you've been on the path for a while, and you ask for support from a friend. They offer to take you out. You go out, get drunk, and do drugs. Or you watch something that distracts you from what's in your mind, or you go out to eat away your feelings. That's perhaps no longer the kind of support you need. Perhaps that friend is representative of an old attachment it's time to graduate from. Maybe what you need now is to talk it out, to breathe, to do something more supportive of where you are now in your growth. It may be time to uplevel your circle to one that is more aligned with where you are and what your new needs are.

Testing Your Material

I've used the phrase "test your material" in this book. Well, relationships are where you get to test your mental strength and tools. You can't protect yourself from the world. You can't isolate yourself. That is not sustainable, and it is not the spiritually sassy way. We have to be in the world, be with people, and continue to grow.

If you've got relationships that you want to nurture but are not totally aligned with where you want to be, go for lunch instead of dinner if you know dinner will lead to drinks. If this is a friend you know you'll go for an unhealthy dinner with, and then for dessert, and then to the bar, and then to the club to get wasted and do drugs until the morning, pick your poison. Do one of those things, not all of them. If you want to quit cigarettes, there's no point in not being friends with anyone who smokes. Next thing you know, you're all alone and protecting yourself from the whole world. This is not the tantric path. You have to be strong enough in yourself that you can still engage with other people, no matter where they are on their path. You can't expect everyone to be on the same page as you—you have to meet them where they are.

And there is no way to be perfect. Instead of quitting everything cold turkey, ask yourself: Is this skillful or unskillful, beneficial or harmful? Ask yourself: Is having three glasses of wine harmful or beneficial? Is having five cigarettes harmful or beneficial? Make a choice. The empowering thing in all of this is, no matter what you decide, you are aware and making the choice rather than acting unconsciously on autopilot. Staying in and avoiding life and people because they trigger you is a form of spiritual bypassing. It is entirely possible to make choices and navigate existing relationships without cutting them off and without sacrificing your progress if you're strong enough inside.

I personally had to leave everyone behind for a while. But at some point, you will reconnect, and that's good because, again, you need to test your material. Remember, everyone's path is different. Some people's trauma with family and friends is so intense that it might take years to mend the relationship before they can ever go back. You can totally still see your friends and people who are rooted in the old ways, but in a new light. It can be as simple as a matter of choice. Instead of going home for every holiday, just go for one. Or maybe you don't want to go for the holidays because the holidays are when everyone is drinking and eating like crap and doing all kinds of unskillful things. Maybe you'd rather go home at a random time of year when you can have more intimate time for connection.

While you've been trying to understand your mind and figure out who you really are in your heart, others have been enjoying the cycle of quick pleasure and pain (suffering) and are fully engaged in their lives. They are enjoying getting high (on gossip, on negativity, on drugs, on alcohol, on toxic relationships). It's not your job to judge, and you don't need to. This is so important. People can also sense a change in you whether or not you talk about it. You might find that people are triggered by *you*. We all want to feel good, and sometimes, when we see others change their lives, it puts a mirror up to our own. Have compassion. Observe, and most importantly, don't judge.

You can evaluate the caliber of your own awakening by noticing if and when triggers arise for you. For example, for a few years I stopped going home for holidays. Instead I'd go at random times of the year, but no matter what, to celebrate, my dad would have a barbecue. People would be drinking and eating meat, and my dad would still offer me alcohol and meat despite knowing that wasn't the path I was on. At first I would get so upset, like, "Hello, you know I'm a vegan! WTF." But slowly, that curriculum evolved, and instead I could have compassion for him. For him, offering me meat and alcohol was a loving gesture. It is a wise person that can give others the benefit of the doubt. No one wants to cause harm or suffering. We all have a natural baseline for compassion. We are compassionate at our core; we must give people the benefit of the doubt and assume kindness. Some might praise you and others might look down upon you. That's okay. It's not about you. It's your work to not take it personally. Don't waste your energy getting angry.

Intentional Socializing

Go to the places that reflect where you are and where you want to be. Go! If you want to be friends and know like-minded people, go to where they are! Show up. Take a risk. Show up looking fabulous. Show up with a beautiful smile. Show up smelling good. Make an effort. Match your external look to your internal freedom. If you're still looking for your spiritually sassy, high-vision tribe at happy hour, you're not gonna find them there, honey. Stop looking for high-vision people at low-vibe places. You gotta go to the high-vision places. Save your money and go to that festival you've been dreaming of going to. Save money and go to that conference you've been wanting to go to. Look for people in the places you wish to be found. Catch yourself when you're spinning into "I'll never find my tribe, I'm so alone." You better believe these kinds of thoughts impact your internal garden, because they're watering old seeds of unworthiness you're trying to set yourself free from. Trust that you're creating the conditions for your beautiful friends to show up. Water new seeds that support this knowing.

External distractions, triggers, and annoying people are always going to be there, but it's all about how we do or don't get taken by them. We won't take everything they're saying personally. We will dance with triggers and annoying people in a whole new way. What they say is a reflection of the quality of their mind; how you react is a reflection of yours.

Sometimes people graduate with you, sometimes they don't, but don't let fifteen years of friendship be ruined over a five-minute fight. Imagine, you're doing so well, you're so lit, you're so awake. You're on the high vision, and suddenly you see your mom, and she knows exactly what to say to piss you off. You lose yourself in anger and think, "OMG, all my work is wasted!" Realize you fell, and pick your fucking ass back up. You have this choice available to you each and every time you fall. Get. Back. Up. When you wallow, you know you have a lot of work to do. When you can bounce back, that's when you know your work is working. Pick your ass up and look fabulous while you do. That's spiritually sassy. And have the courage to admit you fucked up and forgive yourself.

When you're with your friends, do you feel happy? Do you feel inspired? Replenished? Can you be vulnerable? Or do you find yourself gossiping, judging? Do you feel resistance but you go anyway because you feel obligated and that's all you know? The states of mind you cultivate in these moments become your traits, so we need to treat this time preciously and make decisions wisely. Loving friendships and relationships are not about how many gifts you get, but about how you relate to each other's minds and support each other to explore uncharted territories within yourselves. If your inner qualities diminish around your friends, then these are people you have to take a break from. If you are looking for friends, know they are looking for you, too.

The Power of No

Saying no is not rude. Check your intention, though. Is your intention self-preservation, or is it spiritual bypassing? When you say no in order to spiritually bypass some difficult inner work, there's still a bit of wobbliness. Catch the instability, check yourself and your intention, and say no from a place of self-preservation, not a place of fear or avoidance. From the place of self-preservation, you're in your power. From fear, you're in a place where you can leak and harm others and yourself. When you say no intentionally, you teach a lesson. How you spend your time is either high vision or no vision—there's no middle ground. Think about it: time and energy are ultimately the only resources we have.

Using Social Media Responsibly

Let's be honest, social media is a part of life. It's unavoidable. Here are some ways to know if you're using it in a healthy way or if it's time for a break.

Signs you are using social media responsibly and for good:

- You feel inspired by it.
- You're taking action and choosing to make change.
- You're accountable.
- You're speaking the truth.
- You're being vulnerable.
- You're not taking things too seriously.

Signs you're not on social media in a spiritually sassy way, and it's toxic:

- You're constantly comparing.

- You're constantly competing.
- You're leaving mean comments.
- You feel drained when you look at it.
- You're numbing out when you're on it.
- You're using it to distract from your internal chaos.
- You follow low-vibe content.

THE POWER OF SHARING

A powerful way to quiet shame and intrusive thoughts is to share your story. Watch the way people react to your radical honesty. Is there judgment or awe? I bet you'll find that you'll give permission to some and you'll see others who are afraid of your boldness because they're not quite ready yet. Both are okay. When you're in your power, you're not affected by either; you're simply being you and letting your dream emanate from you. This is part of your mission—to take up space and be an inspiration.

Share your story from a place of empowerment. Look at your fucked-up story, what you learned from it, what you did to change it, and who you are now. That in itself is empowering. This is the foundation of a vulnerable conversation. Everybody has obstacles. Everyone will continue to have obstacles, but we're looking to people, actual human beings, who have walked the path and come out on the other side.

By sharing the keys of your personal awakening, you show people around you how to open the door. You can't open the door for someone, but you can give them the keys, show them to the door, and give them some tips for how to open it. But they have to open it and walk through it themselves. You can't go into someone's heart and unlock it. You make the most impact by helping others do their own healing.

When you find a way to share your personal liberation in a creative way, that is when you have landed. Creativity is the default of the heart. You could be a performance artist or you could be an engineer; creativity can touch anyone. It's in the way you speak, the way you carry yourself, the way you engage with others—these are subtle ways to share. Making an impact has nothing to do with the way we're programmed to think; rather, it's simply about passing down your tools.

Reframe Shame

"I'm a piece of shit." "I don't deserve to be happy." "I'm worthless." "No one loves me."

Perhaps you've had thoughts like these. Well, they might continue to show up. You must reframe them as they arise; otherwise, you're going to hide, isolating yourself with your negative self-talk, and that's where shame breeds—in the dark. Shame is the belief that you're bad, unworthy, inadequate, not good enough.

What are three shame narratives that have come up for you? Write them below.

1.

2.

3.

Now reframe the above statements in a more positive way:

1.

2.

3.

Unless we reframe these feelings, our minds will find powerful, sneaky, fucked-up ways to validate them. "Yeah, I *am* a piece of shit!" "I really don't deserve to be happy." "It's true—no one loves me." No. Stop these lies in their tracks. Catch, reframe, and remind yourself that these are mental events and nothing more.

Other things you can do to bring shame to the light:

- Talk about it with a friend or loved one.

- Write about it in your journal.

Stand in Your Full Power

Standing in your power leads you to even more full-power experiences. As this happens, other people may see you as a threat. You may become a trigger for someone, but that has nothing to do with you. Not that you're absolved of taking responsibility for your actions if you hurt someone. Of course not. Just remember that as you change, things shift for those around you, too. You may need to hold space for others in your circle; you may start to see relationships shift. All of this is okay. You just keep doing you, loud and clear. Freedom doesn't happen in a vacuum. We're all connected, so when you get free, you help others get free, too.

When you're in alignment, there's no aftertaste, no residue, no gag reflex when you engage with the world. You have a sense of gratitude, new ideas come up, and there's a feeling of empowerment. This is your cue that your inner values match your actions.

Alignment Prayer

Dear Buddha nature,

Dear part of me that's already awakened,

Dear heart,

Dear universe,

Show me where I am not in alignment

May I bring alignment to those parts

Show me the steps, show me who I have to talk to, show me what I have to do, show me what I have to read in order to bring alignment into my life

I know that I'm always being guided by the exact people, places, and experiences I need to have

I know I am being divinely taken care of every step of the way

I continue to show up in alignment for the highest good of all

I know that true alignment is just one breath away, one pause away

I know that I am always connected to this part of myself, my Buddha nature, my infinite potential for complete awakening

I know this part of me is filled with wisdom, complete and utter joy, love, and compassion

RADICAL ACCEPTANCE

I see radical acceptance as the umbrella of both radical self-compassion and self-care. Practicing radical self-compassion is acknowledging we all have flaws, that we've all made mistakes, but we're not allowing these things to dictate the quality of our days or the quality of our lives. The word *compassion* in Sanskrit means compassion for oneself and compassion for others, but in the English dictionary, *compassion* means only compassion for others. So, a new word needed to be created: *self-compassion*. This language shows the extra layer of work we have to do to think of ourselves in a caring and loving way. Compassion fundamentally means the wish for ourselves and others to be free of suffering.

Self-compassion and self-care are like taking a pause whenever you're beating yourself up over something that happened—when you coulda, woulda, shoulda said this or done that, when you're holding grudges, when you're feeling remorse or regret. Putting radical acceptance, radical self-compassion, and radical self-care into action means that you are choosing not to cling to what's already happened. You allow yourself to acknowledge that you feel regret for a moment, but you don't hold on. Instead you choose the path of freedom and wisdom. Radical self-compassion doesn't mean that you bypass the mistakes you've made; rather, it means that no matter how many times you fall, you are committed to getting back up and being there for yourself each and every time. You are committed to your liberation.

Before we can have compassion for others, we need to have compassion for ourselves. If our own internal resources are depleted, we can't even pick up on the suffering of others; instead we see others' suffering as a trigger rather than an opportunity to offer help. So, radical self-compassion and service: these are two sides of the same coin.

Radical Self-Care

It is your job to be a solution-based individual. It is your job to choose carefully how you are impacting the world around you. Sometimes self-care means checking in with yourself and asking, "Can I be in public today?" "Can I go out and interact with people?" "Am I leaking, projecting, and inflicting pain onto others?" This is important. If you're going out into the world and coloring your experience with your mental delusions and negative emotions, then honey, go back home. Your choice to go home is an act of self-care. You're tuning into your heart, discerning what's best for yourself and others, and taking action.

Radical Service

This is where it all comes together, the point of it all. How fun would it be to awaken, only to find yourself all alone? You've crossed the river of suffering, all the way to the other shore, and . . . you're the only one there? You'd be lonely, and it would be so boring. Imagine being on a boat by yourself, looking down at everyone drowning, and thinking, *Hahahaha, you're all down there suffering* and not helping them get on the boat. Being of service is an innate part of the path.

I do not want you to think, as so many of my students have, "I'm not doing enough. I need to be doing more." It's not true. Your choice to do this self-liberating work is impacting everybody. The next realization that occurs is that you MUST give something back to the world, that you MUST beautify the world. When you start to beautify your mind, you beautify the world.

When you feel the pull to serve, don't hold back. When you want to give in any way, then gift, compliment, don't hold back. You may be thinking, "OMG I feel so good when I gift." You want to continue to do it because it feels good. Helper's high is a real thing. You get a little high when you help someone. But if your next moment is kinder, more peaceful, and more present, then you're deepening the purity of your intention. At some point, you're not sharing or giving to get high; you're doing it to get free. When we talk about *ahimsa*, or nonviolence, we're not necessarily only talking about you not punching people in the face. We're talking about not inflicting harm with your thoughts, your words, and your actions.

On a really basic level, just know this: when you empower others, you empower yourself, and when you help others, you help yourself. On a heart level, we are the same. You must see others as you. By teaching the tools that have helped you, you create more healing within yourself. When you help someone to forgive, you help yourself to forgive. We are mirrors, people! And from a selfish perspective, helping others just feels good. And there is nothing wrong with feeling good.

YOUR JOYFUL MISSION

As we have discussed, joy is the language of the heart. We must become fluent in this language. It must become our new default. I want you to get to a place where you see and hear the world through a lens of beauty, awe, and wonder. There's a deep sense of connection to what reality truly is simply because you realize that the quality of your experiences is totally determined by the quality of your mind and your connection to your heart.

This connection is what's dictating the amount of beauty you see in the world, the amount of compassion you're putting out in the world, the amount of joy and laughter and play you're experiencing in this dance with the world. You realize how deeply interconnected we are, so when you think about your dream, your mission, your purpose, you realize it's much bigger than just you. Then you start thinking, "I need to be a yoga teacher, a wellness teacher, a life coach, a wellness writer . . ." No. It doesn't have to be so linear. You can be a chef, a jewelry designer, a fashion designer, a carpenter, a farmer, a waiter. You can be whatever the fuck you want to be! As long as you are doing your work, purifying your mind, the job you do doesn't matter.

There is no spiritual profession. There is only a spiritual heart. If your heart is open and your mind is concentrated, everything and anything you do will be an expression of this inner alignment. Everything you do, everything you touch, is sacred, and everyone who comes into contact with that depth in you will be impacted. My definition of *truth* is a deep connection to the heart. When someone's operating from that place of high vision, it is undeniable.

You can feel it—when you look at a piece of jewelry or an item of clothing made from this place, or you get served by someone at a restaurant who's operating from that place, or you look at a piece of art or watch a film or listen to a song, it is undeniable. You know truth. Your body knows truth. Whatever you do, you can choose to do it from a place of altruism, from a place of deep compassion. More and more creativity will continue to arise. More and more, what you put into the world will be of benefit.

Everyone is worthy of a high-vision life. When you're living in the high vision, you're living with joy. It's funny—all my teachers have had a sense of humor in their teaching style. Even the Dalai Lama is constantly making people laugh. You can gauge someone's level of awakening by how joyous their presence is, how bright their smile is. It's about the energy that comes from their being. Joy is contagious.

I had a rare opportunity to meet a spiritual master, who spent twelve years in a cave in the Himalayas. One of the things I reflected back to her was my gratitude for her style of teaching. She reminded me to be joyous, and not to take things too seriously. She was constantly making us laugh. There are these six *paramitas* (the *six perfections* in Tibetan Buddhism), and on the day we met, she said to me that there should be a seventh paramita and it should be joy. How amazing. So much of being spiritually sassy is about being joyous. The other perfections: generosity, morality, patience, strength, concentration, and wisdom. The seventh is JOY.

10

The High Vision

Step 8: Stay slaying.

Just like exercise keeps the body fit, an internal work-out program is necessary for staying in shape spiritually and psychologically. And, just like we lose motivation for going to the gym, we need a system in place to help us stay motivated to be spiritually and psychologically healthy. It's important to have reminders of your "why," regular practice, and a support system to ensure your mind is clear and heart awakened in service of the highest good of all, and not your fears. This chapter is about maintenance mode—the skills and wisdom you can always fall back on.

THE FOUR PILLARS OF MAINTENANCE[1]

Congratulations, you've made it to the maintenance phase! There are four key pillars when it comes to spiritual maintenance: spiritual practice, flow, exercise, and relationships. Committing to nurture these areas will ensure you stay on the path.

Spiritual Practice

This is internal gardening time. Sit with yourself, connect with the stillness in the center of your being, open up to the silence in your heart, and listen! The most powerful way to do this is in meditation, a concentration technique, one that guides you to simply gather all the energy of your mind into the feeling of the breath in your body. Distractions will come, the mind will wander, and all you need to do is come back to the breath over and over. So simple! Start with five minutes and build from there. The important thing is that you do this every day. Mantra, prayers, and affirmations are supplementary to the core work of mind training. A concentrated mind is a happy mind, and a happy mind gives you direct access to your heart.

Flow

This speaks to what you do every day toward your heart's mission. By now you know that you must share your gifts, and sharing your gifts in small or big ways is part of your daily maintenance. Make space for flow, or at least, make space to find what brings you closer to this state: explore curiosities and learn, because your curiosities become your passion and passion leads to a purposeful life. This is an essential part of spirituality.

Exercise

Physical health supports mental health, and vice versa. Likewise, physical health supports spiritual progress. Self-care in the form of exercise, no matter what it is, is a powerful act of self-love. When you take care of yourself, you normalize self-care, and your whole body will support your healing.

Relationships

Connection and belonging are needs of the heart. When our relationships reflect these feelings back to us, we are on the right track. Do your relationships nourish you? Do they mirror back to you a high vision? Look at your relationships and see them as an extension of both how you heal and how you give back. Our relationships are where we can experience the power of both giving love and receiving love; feeling good, and making others feel good; belonging, and making others feel they belong. Relationships are key because in them, we have the privilege of *acting* on love and *being* expressions of love.

Every day, we are presented with so many opportunities to choose to nurture these areas of life. Trust that if you do your part, the universe will take care of the rest. These are natural laws, as natural as gravity. We have to trust that these laws are setting us free, and that when we do our work, growth happens.

Emotional and Spiritual Fitness

Emotional and spiritual fitness, just like any fitness plan, requires . . . a plan. How many days a week do you need to work out to stay healthy and sane? What do you need to eat to be healthy and sane? Do you pack a salad for work every day? Do you work out three times a week consistently? What is your emotional and spiritual plan for everyday life, seven days a week? A commitment is required if you want to maintain your progress.

This is real life. Let's not pretend that we become aware and suddenly we're superhuman and nothing affects us anymore. Nope. You're still gonna be an emotional human and things are still gonna piss you off. This is where the everyday practice comes in. Every single day is spiritual practice. Every single day is an opportunity to pause before automatically self-medicating. Eventually, your brain will catch on. It will learn that there is no lion. But you have to lead the way.

Emotional fitness, at its base level, is preventive care. We have to look at our internal worlds daily. But through habit and conditioning, we do such a fantastic job at ignoring the parts of ourselves we cannot (or don't want to) see.

So that is what emotional and spiritual fitness is all about: taking care of the part of ourselves that we cannot see.

Otherwise, negative feelings accumulate, thoughts populate, and you react blindly when triggered: "Go! Do something! Make it go away!" And so you drink some wine or you start scrolling through social media to numb yourself, or you eat ice cream or smoke a joint. As harmless as these activities might seem, when done with the intention of avoiding discomfort, they don't teach the brain to self-soothe. Instead they teach the brain to find an external fix the second you get a distress signal. On a spiritual level, each time you react blindly, you are once again nurturing the karmic seeds in your garden so these tendencies will continue to prevail.

Making a Plan

The mental plan you need to put in place has to do with triggers, numbing, and avoidance, because these are the things that lead to downward spirals and unsupportive behaviors brought on by uncomfortable feelings. Below, or on a separate piece of paper, I want you to write down your top three triggers. Your trigger might be a feeling, like sadness or anger, or it might be a situation you find yourself in often. Next, write down your usual numbing or avoidance behavior, and then write down what you commit to do instead the next time this trigger comes up. This way, you get familiar with your own everyday patterns. The next time one starts to play itself out, you can be prepared with another response, one that sets you free.

Trigger: _____

Numbing behavior: _____

Avoidance behavior: _____

Spiritually sassy behavior: _____

Trigger: _____

Numbing behavior: _____

Avoidance behavior: _____

Spiritually sassy behavior: _____

Trigger: _____

Numbing behavior: _____

Avoidance behavior: _____

Spiritually sassy behavior: _____

When you do this enough times, you initiate change and purification at every level—physical, psychological, and spiritual. Eventually you'll get these new mental habits into your DNA, but until then, try to see every day as an opportunity to practice your new tool and apply your new mindset. Make this work for you, but know that it requires commitment every single day. It requires checking in with your values, checking in with your heart.

Establishing Inner Stability

Inner stability will eventually become your default. A simple and powerful way for you to know if you are nourishing this pillar is to see how often you are taken by distractions, whether internal or external—how often you reach for the sweets, cigarettes, alcohol, for the gossiping, for the things that you did in the past that kept you stuck.

Notice how you handle triggers. A powerful sign that you are moving forward, toward complete liberation, is you are able to catch yourself when you are blaming external events for how you are feeling inside, and instead you redirect your attention and look inward. Triggers are signals pointing us to where we need healing.

Quick Practice: How Am I Doing?

A simple yet powerful tool I want you to start using is a self-check-in. This takes you out of autopilot mode and makes checking in a new default.

On a scale of 1-10, how am I doing?

1	2	3	4	5	6	7	8	9	10

I feel like shit   Healthy and stable

Ask yourself: What do I need right now?

Practice really listening to yourself. Make an effort to nourish whatever is lacking in a healthy way. You deserve it. Take joy in answering your needs with acts of loving self-care.

Spirituality Is Life

Spirituality is not only in a yoga studio, it is not only at a meditation retreat, and it is not only in an online course. It is not only in this book. All of these things and places offer tools and practices, but the next-level work happens in the world, in your real life, when you are brushing up against hardship and stress and difficult people and pain. How do you act? How will you act differently? This is what counts, not how many retreats you've done. Your life is the truest teacher, and how you respond to life is the spiritual practice.

Some teachers have said that all of our problems stem from how we relate to others. While relationships can cause problems, they can also heal. People are a big part of life, and you need a spiritual team, like a sangha, just like you need doctors, therapists, and trainers. Who are your cheerleaders? Which of your friends will help you stay accountable? Who will engage in healthy activities with you?

In my main team, my inner circle consists of my sister, my brother, and a few close friends—who, funnily enough, I met online as I started to share more and more in a public setting. This is a testament to what happens when you share your story and tools with others and give back. You find your tribe. It will happen.

The people on your team are reflectors. They are so bright because they're reflecting back to you all of your brightness. These are people who are continuously being your loudest cheerleaders and your biggest tough-love supporters.

Life offers us opportunities every moment to be free. Choose freedom more often. That's the whole idea. You got this.

Live Every Day Like It's Your Last

I know it sounds cliché, but actually doing it is so useful: remember to show up every single day like it is your last day. I remind myself to do this as a tool for waking up, all the time. I know it sounds kind of morbid, but we need to internalize the truth that each and every one of us at some point will die—our loved ones, our most dear ones, our enemies, our lovers . . . every single human being on Earth right now will die at some point. Think about the legacy you want to leave behind. Do you want to be remembered for fitting nicely into a box, or for being the person that showed up to life and inspired people?

Your Last Breath Meditation

Take a comfortable position lying down with your eyes closed. Bring your awareness to the sensation of the breath, focusing on this ordinary process that keeps you alive.

Now visualize yourself on your deathbed. Get into the feeling that these are your last moments on Earth; feel death coming closer. Feel the loss of everything you wanted but didn't get, everything you tried to achieve but did not. Feel the death of your aspirations and dreams.

Feel the unfinished conversations. What did you want to say to your family and friends or someone you have been fighting with?

Stay connected to the feeling of death approaching. What are you still holding back? What are you not expressing honestly about yourself? Allow these answers to come to you. This is your last opportunity to come clean with yourself. Get deep into the feeling. What have you been lying to yourself about? How have you self-sabotaged your success? Allow these answers to come to you, too.

Feel the last breaths of your precious life. Take another breath. What would you like to say to your loved ones? What would you like to say to yourself?

May this practice make clear what is most important to you in your life. To come out of this meditation, take a deep breath, open your eyes, and rejoice in being alive.

EMOTIONAL FITNESS FOR LIFE

We need to have mechanisms in our spiritual fanny pack for processing feelings and emotions as they arise. And remember, not every feeling, emotion, and thought that arises is an indicator of the truth. What indicates the truth is your response to them when they arise. And your response to them is based on the depth of your connection to the heart.

When you're emotionally fit, things don't get to you the way they did in the past; you're not taken in by every single thought, every single emotion, every single feeling, every single distraction. From your inner world through to the outer world, you can remain in a state of equanimity and loving awareness. In that state of awareness is where the heart and inner wisdom and light arises, burns, diffuses, and releases the grip of our conditioning.

The spiritual path is not about getting anything. Rather, it's about removing things. In this process of removing things, we remember our true, awakened nature, which is perfect and magical. And when we have access to this true nature, we become aware. With this awareness we realize that things aren't how they appear—they are much better, and their potential is endless.

I find the essence of the Serenity Prayer, which is recited in Alcoholics Anonymous and other twelve-step programs, to be so beautiful. To me, it gets at the heart of our everyday, moment-to-moment decision-making on the path, this discerning what's real and what's not. I find this adapted version so helpful, and maybe you will too:

I've made peace with the things I cannot change. I have the courage to change the things I can, and I have the wisdom to know the difference.

YOU AS F*CK

You are deserving, you are the shit, you are loved, you have all the tools you need—the community you need, the internal resources you need to be the absolute best You. And if you don't in this moment, trust that whatever is missing is coming to you. You are enough.

For me, the embodiment of doing me AF is not giving a fuck. I mean this in the most empowering and aware way. Giving zero fucks is screaming, "I am enough!" Whatever you are doing that supports your heart wisdom, do it loud, bold, and sassy. Giving zero fucks doesn't mean you don't care about the world—on the contrary. Not giving a fuck means you have a singular focus on taking good care of you, which means believing in you, having your own back, not depending on the validation of others, and freely doing what you want, being with who you want, and loving what you want. This means you are no longer driven by what others might think. *That* is what you give zero fucks about. *That* is doing you AF. It is a liberating act. What people think of you has nothing to do with you.

A big moment for me, as far as doing me as fuck, was when I started posting my dance videos on Instagram. I was so afraid of what people were going to say, because what is a spiritual teacher who is supposed to be all *namaste* and wearing white doing dancing? Oh my goodness, from my conditioned perspective, dancing was so not what a spiritual teacher was supposed to be doing. But it was what I wanted because I knew I was doing it for me, my heart.

Once I understood that dancing was deeply rooted in a purification practice for me, I realized it was an important tool to share with others. I was terrified of what people would say, what the response would be. The feedback I received was that people found it inspiring, that it encouraged others to dance and allow themselves to be freer. Wow! People were in fact very open to seeing a spiritual teacher through a different lens. This taught me that showing people another view is part of my work and what I came to share. You can be impactful and be spiritual being exactly who you are.

Embodying Inspiration Meditation

Bring to mind someone who inspires you, someone whose qualities you admire.

Let yourself feel joy for the fact that this wise being has actualized and internalized all these qualities and is living their truth.

Now envision yourself embodying all these same qualities.

Visualize how you walk through the world, how you talk to people, how you see yourself, how you see the world once you have embodied the very qualities you admire.

You Belong

My love, wherever you are, know you belong. If where you are is not where you'd like to be, ask yourself what is to be learned here and make a plan for the future without getting caught up in the self-doubt of the conditioned mind. Go to the heart and listen to the voice that believes in you, and remember, moving forward moment by moment is freedom. One foot in front of the other, little by little. Every choice, each moment can lead you to freedom.

On the flipside, when you are making progress and the big bad Not Enough voices come (and they will for a while), you will know better. Cultivating awareness and choice is a lifelong journey of acknowledging, again and again, *I am aware that I am having this thought but I am choosing to move forward anyway.* The self-belief muscle gets stronger as you grow. When I feel imposter syndrome coming on, or when I feel doubt creeping in, whenever an opportunity comes along and I start to feel like, "Who the hell do I think I am?" I just whisper: *I'm enough, I belong*, until the doubting voice subsides. This is the constant work of believing in yourself and staying the path.

My journey to belonging and not giving a fuck was certainly not easy. I grew up in a family that valued sameness. Anything outside of a narrow definition of socially acceptable and normal was scary . . . wrong. Insert little Sah. As a boy, I spent much of my time feeling overwhelmed and confused. I remember asking whoever/whatever was listening to me, "Make me normal, please make me normal."

Looking back at that little boy who desired something that does not really exist (normality), who didn't feel he belonged and felt as though he himself was wrong, I am overcome with compassion for him. This shame is strong, people. We have to realize that this stuff lingers and tries to creep in, so we must skillfully say no to stories of "not enough," "don't belong," "wrong," because they could not be further from the truth.

I know many of you will be able to relate. We each have our own stories. I was desperately seeking belonging, but I didn't yet know that what I needed was not external validation, but to feel belonging within myself, to feel at home and relaxed in my own body. This is why the spiritual work is so transformative. When you learn that where you've always belonged is in your own heart and find a true home there, everything changes. When you learn it is safe and you begin to feel at home in your body, you realize that here on Earth, you do in fact belong; here in this human experience, we all belong, and we are deeply interconnected.

You can always remember the recipe for belonging with this acronym. Repeat these affirmations anytime you need a reminder:

B Brave - *I step outside of my conditioning and accept myself with bravery*

E Effortless - *Loving and believing in myself is effortless*

L Legendary - *I am aware of my potential; I am legendary*

O Open - *My heart is open; sharing who I am heals me and you*

N Nourished - *Deeply nourishing myself is what I do*

G Good - *I am innately good*

When you feel disconnected, just noticing that feeling is a huge progression on the spiritual path. That is your heart nudging you to reconnect. When you feel bored, lonely, stuck, you can learn to see these feeling states not as who you are, but instead as nudges from your heart sending you the courage to act and change your life. Even as you notice those feelings and don't get caught up in them, that is a form of belonging. In the moment of being aware that those feelings are impermanent and not you, you are touching belonging. You feel the pull from your heart; follow it, trust it.

You Have Everything You Need

You may still be asking: "Am I good enough? Do I have what it takes? Do I deserve the things I want? Am I worthy?" But guess what? That's just the conditioned mind talking to itself all day; you don't have to engage in every conversation. It is your job to observe and choose, every single day, every single moment, to say yes to You. *Yes, I am good enough. Yes, I am good. Yes, I am enough. Yes, I deserve. Yes, I am worthy.* This is the Work, my friend. Every day, each moment. It is the Work to stand up for what is true about you day in and day out, to reside in the part of you that is always free, the part of you that *is* love, so that you may have joy as a baseline and help others have the same.

May all the practices and wisdom in this book be of service to you on your path toward freedom. May you awaken joy. May you be free. May you work to benefit others.

My love, freedom is possible.

11

More Meditations, Prayers, and Mantras for Your Journey

Congratulations, my love. I am so proud of you for making it to the end of this book. You have worked so hard and made so much progress. Now your continued success depends on you committing to practicing regularly. I've included some of my very favorite (and most effective) meditations, mantras, and prayers. Please use them often. Enjoy! I love you.

Primal Screaming

Yelling at someone because you're angry is not the same thing as screaming to let out frustration. This is a healing process to move thoughts and feelings that are trapped. It's mainly to be used when you're hooked and also, once in a while, to release pent-up emotions that are stuck in your body. Primal scream therapy is actually a legit form of psychotherapy for treating anxiety, trauma, and stress.

Inhale deeply, and then let out a really strong scream. Do this three times.

Purpose of Life Prayer (adapted from Shantideva[1])

This is something that I read quite frequently. It's a great way to reconnect with the purpose of life. Read it as often as you can. Try to incorporate this prayer into your daily practice. It reminds us of the ultimate goal.

May I become now and forever a protector of those without protection, a guide for those who have lost their way, a ship for those with oceans to cross, a bridge for those with rivers to cross, a sanctuary for those in danger, a lamp for those without light, a place of refuge for those without shelter, a servant for all in need, as long as space endures, for as long as living beings remain. Until then, may I too abide to dispel the miseries of the world.

Tantric Buddhist Mantras

These mantras are extremely potent. If they don't resonate with you right away, then they are not for you right now. Move on. Maybe come back later.

Warning: When you repeat these mantras, it's like putting your finger in an outlet. Some strange things may happen. Be aware and practice responsibly.

Medicine Buddha mantra

The purpose of this mantra is to heal physical illness. There are a couple of ways to do this. First, you can repeat the mantra 108 times to yourself. Or, you can repeat this mantra 108 times over a glass of water and either give the water to someone who is sick or drink it yourself.

Tayatha om bekandze bekandze maha bekandze radza samudgate soha.

Here is how you say it: Taya-te om bekan-ze bekan-ze maha bekan-ze raja samu-gate so-ha.

Manjushri mantra

Chanting this mantra enhances wisdom and fosters a stable mind. Use it as you put in place skills learned from this book.

Om Am Rah Pa Dza Na Dhi

Here is how you say it: Om a ra pa cha na dee-hee.

Repeat 108 times a day anytime you need help learning or seeing things clearly, with wisdom.

Vajrasattva mantra

This mantra is one of the most powerful and fast-acting that I've encountered. I got the initiation recently in Nepal. This is an expedited karmic cleanse and, just as with any cleanse, what you're processing must come out, so be prepared to purge.

Om vajrasattva hum

Here is how you say it: Om vajra-sat-fa hum.

Chant this twenty-eight times a day.

I do this every night before bed. This mantra cleanses any unwholesome deeds accumulated during the day through mind, body, and speech so we don't hold on to them and bring them into the next day.

Green Tara mantra

This is one of my most favorite mantras. It is a huge heart anchor for me. I'm constantly repeating it in my mind throughout the day. I even have Green Tara, the emanation deity of universal compassion, enlightenment, and virtuous performances, tattooed on my left arm.

Om tare tutare ture soha

Here is how you say it: Om tar-ay tutar-ay tur-ay swoha.

This mantra has many benefits and translations. Here is the one I love the most:

May all beings everywhere be free of mental and physical suffering and all of its causes, and may all beings everywhere have happiness and all of its causes.

Try repeating this mantra 108 times at once, or throughout the day. Doing so frees you from destructive feelings of pride, ignorance, jealousy, hatred, stubbornness, attachment, disturbing doubts, and greed.

Mantras for Ordinary Life

How much time do you waste going from app to app to music to Instagram? Instead of distracting yourself, use everyday life and idle time to get into a deep purification process through the following mantras. We make them extraordinary by attaching to them our intention to be liberated.

Walking on the street
Offer a silent blessing to each person you pass. Instead of passing each person and judging cute, ugly, want, don't want, sexy, not sexy, black, white—all the unconscious biases and prejudice that run automatically in our minds—we can start to purify our conditioning. Practice silently wishing everyone you come in contact with, *May you be happy* or *May you live with ease*.

Showering, washing dishes, or doing laundry
When doing these activities you can repeat this mantra:
For the highest good of all, I wash away all thoughts, feelings, emotions, situations, beings, and energies that are no longer in service to my awakening.

Eating prayer
Before you eat, repeat this prayer: *Thank you everyone everywhere who created the conditions for me to have this food—Mother Nature, everyone at the farm, everyone at the store, everyone everywhere who created the financial conditions for me to be able to buy this food. This food is healing, grounding, this food is an offering of abundance to all sentient beings who don't have food at this moment.*

By generating this wish for all to have wholesome food, you are awakening courage and discipline within yourself to do more to help others.

Waiting in line
We tend to drift away when we're waiting. Instead, use this idle time to bring clarity and calm to your mind. Repeat: *In the now I am free, in the present I am free.*

Writing Prompt: Right Now I Feel . . .

Use this anytime you're hooked and taken in by your feelings.

Set a timer for fifteen to twenty minutes. Grab paper and a pen. Start by writing, "Right now I feel," and continue from there to free write.

When you come to a place where you think you have nothing else to say, take a deep breath and go again: "Right now I feel . . ."

Death Meditation

Do this as often as you can. We're going to be using the thought process in a very creative way as a support to develop wisdom.

To begin, take a comfortable seat on a chair, feet flat, or on a cushion, whatever you like.

Take a few long, deep breaths.

Now rest your energy on the tip of your nose.

Trace the breath going in through the nose and out through the nose for a few moments. Then begin the following meditation.

Inevitability of death

For each line below, you are instructed to use the inner dialogue to have a conversation with yourself. If you drift off into fantasy or to-do lists, come back. Open each statement with:

"I acknowledge that . . ."

Everyone has to die.

Everyone I know will die.

My life span is decreasing continuously.

Even as I do this practice, I am closer to my own death.

The amount of time in my life I have to develop the mind and uncover my heart is very small, so I acknowledge the importance of practicing internal transformation because soon enough, I'll be dead.

Human life expectancy is uncertain.

There are many causes of death.

I might die in a car accident, from disease, in my sleep; or I may get shot.

The human body is fragile; it is an extremely powerful temple, but at the same time it is susceptible to accidents and disease.

Only insight and wisdom can help me during the time of death.

My possessions cannot help, no matter how much money or stuff I have accumulated; none of it matters because I will be gone. All of us. Loved ones, enemies. Everyone will die.

At the end of the day, no one can help, not even our loved ones. When it's my time to go I will go. We will all die.

Our bodies cannot help. Our bodies get sick, they age, and then we die.

As we close this practice, take a few moments to notice how you feel. Thank yourself for practicing and carry the insights with you.

Writing Exercise: Confession

In a journal or other safe space, I invite you to write out a confession. There is tremendous healing power in confessing the harm you've done to yourself and other people. Just reading it out loud can be so powerful. You don't need to share it or even save it. But, when you're finished, read it to yourself and reflect on it. I invite you to throw it out, burn it, or cut it up into many little pieces when finished. This practice helps bring out past harm from hiding and into the light; when it's hiding, it will leak out from you in other ways. Add some forgiveness, and refer to chapter 4 for more tools.

Wisdom Meditation

In this practice, we are going to use our thoughts as an ally, as a way to reflect upon and discover the nature of the purified mind, which is the spiritual heart. So much of our suffering comes from a place of disconnection with the heart, but wisdom can help us reconnect. Let's begin.

Gently close your eyes and sit up with intentionality and grace.

Rest your attention on the feeling of your breath, perhaps at the tip of your nose or the bottom of your belly.

Take a few long, deep breaths, in and out.

Recall a time when you got into an argument with somebody.

With the situation and the person in mind, reflect on the following:

People can change.

No one is innately bad or wrong.

Just like you, they are changing and growing.

The experience doesn't define you and it doesn't define them.

How people react to you is out of your control.

Even if you are wise, kind, compassionate, and calm, other people's behavior is out of your control.

Visualize the same argument, but now see it with a more expanded and generous view.

There are no accidents and no coincidences.

Your past actions created the situation in order for you to learn.

Their perception is valid and your perception is valid.

Being right or wrong is irrelevant.

It's only a problem because you attached meaning to it.

Allow yourself to see it as an opportunity for growth, not as a problem.

As we close this practice, take a few moments to notice how you feel. Thank yourself for practicing and carry the insights with you.

Ha Breath

This breathwork practice is a very powerful way to release toxic stress.

To begin, set a timer for ninety seconds.

Sitting or standing, breathe in and raise both arms up to the sky.

As you breathe out, lower both arms, your elbows gently touching the sides of your ribcage. Say "HA!"

On a quick tempo, breathe in and out, raising the arms on the in breath and lowering them on the out breath.

Your fingers are active, palms facing out.

HA! HA! HA!

Left Nostril Breathing

Breathing in and out through the left nostril for three minutes, you can reclaim agency of your nervous system and give it direction instead of being at its mercy. Instead of cortisol, adrenaline, fight/flight/freeze, you can bring in a sense of rest and relaxation.

Bring your right hand to your face.

With your thumb, close your right nostril.

Now, breathing through only the left nostril, inhale for a count of four and exhale for a count of six. Do this for up to three minutes.

Kapalbhati

This practice is from the yogic scriptures. *Kapalbhati* means "skull shining." I've used this during some of my deepest and darkest times of depression. It helps to unhook you from believing your thoughts, feelings, and emotions. Do this for ninety seconds.

Breathe out a forceful exhalation from your nose.

Keep forcefully exhaling, and the in breath will happen on its own. Breathe this way for a few breaths—back-to-back, short and powerful exhales.

Notes

Chapter 2: The Sassy Foundation

1. Bob Weinhold, "Epigenetics: The Science of Change," *Environmental Health Perspectives* 114, 3 (2006): A160-7, doi:10.1289/ehp.114-a160.

2. "HeartMath Science," HeartMath Institute, heartmath.org/science (accessed October 18, 2019).

Chapter 3: The Current Story of You

1. Remez Sasson, "How Many Thoughts Does Your Mind Think in One Hour?" Success Consciousness Blog, successconsciousness.com/blog/inner-peace /how-many-thoughts-does-your-mind-think-in-one -hour (accessed October 18, 2019).

2. Lion's Roar Staff, "What Are the Four Foundations of Mindfulness?" *Lion's Roar*, June 13, 2018, lionsroar.com /what-are-the-four-foundations-of-mindfulness.

3. J. Hettema, J. Steele, and W. R. Miller, "Motivational Interviewing," *Annual Review of Clinical Psychology* 1 (2005): 91–111.

4. Questions adapted from Center for Substance Abuse Treatment, "Enhancing Motivation for Change in Substance Use Disorder Treatment," *Treatment Improvement Protocol (TIP) 35*. Rockville, MD: Substance Abuse and Mental Health Services Administration, October 2019.

5. "What Is Neuroplasticity?" *Brainworks: Train Your Mind,* brainworksneurotherapy.com /what-neuroplasticity (accessed October 18, 2019).

6. Margaret Jaworski, "The Negativity Bias: Why the Bad Stuff Sticks and How to Overcome It," *Psycom,* May 23, 2019, psycom.net/negativity-bias (accessed October 18, 2019).

7. Kerry J. Ressler, "Amygdala Activity, Fear, and Anxiety: Modulation by Stress," *Biological Psychiatry* 67, 12 (2010): 1117-9, doi:10.1016/j.biopsych.2010.04.027.

8. "Self-Talk Diary" and "Replacing Limiting Beliefs" exercises adapted from Aaron T. Beck, *The Anxiety and Worry Workbook: The Cognitive Behavioral Solution,* 1st ed. (New York: The Guilford Press, 2011).

9. Sethanne Howard and Mark W. Crandall, "Post-Traumatic Stress Disorder: What Happens in the Brain?" *Journal of the Washington Academy of Sciences* 93, 3 (2007): 1–17, jstor.org/stable/24536468.

10. Gretchen Lidicker, "Could Strengthening Your Vagus Nerve Be The Secret to Crushing Your Anxiety?" *Mindbodygreen,* September 30, 2019, mindbodygreen.com /articles/the-vagus-nerve-anxiety-how-to-strengthen-it.

11. Tiffany A. Ito, Jeff T. Larsen, Kyle N. Smith, and John T. Cacioppo, "Negative Information Weighs More Heavily on the Brain: The Negativity Bias in Evaluative Categorizations," *Journal of Personality and Social Psychology* 75, 4 (October 2002), doi:10.7551 /mitpress/3077.003.0041.

12. John A. Sturgeon and Alex J. Zautra, "Social Pain and Physical Pain: Shared Paths to Resilience," *Pain Management* 6, 1 (2016): 63–74, doi:10.2217/pmt.15.56.

Chapter 4: Forgiveness Boot Camp

1. Loren Toussaint, Everett L. Worthington, and David R. Williams, *Forgiveness and Health: Scientific Evidence and Theories Relating Forgiveness to Better Health* (New York: Springer, 2015).

2. Douglas J. Bremner, "Traumatic Stress: Effects on the Brain," *Dialogues in Clinical Neuroscience* 8, 4 (2006): 445–61.

3. Amy F. T. Arnsten et al., "The Effects of Stress Exposure on Prefrontal Cortex: Translating Basic Research into Successful Treatments for Post-Traumatic Stress Disorder," *Neurobiology of Stress* 1 (2015): 89–99, doi:10.1016/j.ynstr.2014.10.002.

4. Jennifer Berry, "Endorphins: Effects and How to Increase Levels," *Medical News Today*, February 6, 2018, medicalnewstoday.com/articles/320839.php (accessed October 18, 2019).

5. Dr. Siri Carpenter, "That Gut Feeling," *American Psychological Association*, September 2012, apa.org /monitor/2012/09/gut-feeling (accessed October 18, 2019).

Chapter 5: The New Story of You

1. Ram Dass, quotecatalog.com/quote/ram-dass-i -would-like-my-N70EZRp (accessed December 21, 2019).

Chapter 6: Be Your Own Guru

1. Steven Kotler, "The Passion Recipe: Four Steps To Total Fulfillment," *Forbes Magazine*, October 8, 2015, forbes.com/sites/stevenkotler/2015/03/27/the-passion -recipe-four-steps-to-total-fulfillment/#6abd69d6bb41.

2. Steven Kotler, "Flow States and Creativity," *Psychology Today*, February 25, 2014, psychologytoday.com/us/blog/the-playing-field /201402/flow-states-and-creativity.

Chapter 8: Overcome the Fear of Being Amazing

1. Lion's Roar Staff, "What Are the Eight Worldly Concerns?" *Lion's Roar*, Feb 13, 2016, lionsroar.com /buddhism-by-the-numbers-the-eight-worldly -concerns (accessed December 28, 2019).

Chapter 10: The High Vision

1. The four pillars of maintenance are adapted from the curriculum of the Institute of Integrative Nutrition, integrativenutrition.com/.

Chapter 11: More Meditations, Prayers, and Mantras for Your Journey

1. Shantideva, "Shantideva Prayer," Unitarian Universalist Association, from *The Bodhisattvacaryāvatāra (Guide to the Bodhisattva's Way of Life)*, uua.org /worship/words/quote-reading/shantideva-quote (accessed January 10, 2020).

Acknowledgments

A huge thanks to my agent Coleen O'Shea for your vision and your loving support. Thank you to my editor, Diana Ventimiglia, for being a champion for the book throughout this journey, and for all the times I needed a cheerleader. Thanks to everyone at Sounds True for believing in this book and bringing it into the world. I want to thank Melissa Valentine for your hard work, your patience and kindness through this process, and for your beautiful inquiry into my mind that insured I brought the best, most clear heart wisdom through.

Tenzin Chogkyi, one of my teachers who helped me simplify some of the most complex teachings in the book—thank you for your wisdom.

I want to thank Tenzin Palmo for reinforcing the importance of teaching about joy. I'm so grateful for His Holiness the 14th Dalai Lama for being an example of who we can become. I want to acknowledge Lama Zopa Rinpoche who saw something in me before I saw it in myself.

I'm so grateful to my friend Karen Chodron, for her teachers, and for the wisdom in her that is reflected back to me. I would like to thank Venerable Sarah Thresher and our guides who made visiting the holy caves of Guru Rinpoche possible. Ezra Johnson, you were instrumental in encouraging me to always write my truth and be myself. Thank you, Jackie Cantwell, Ian Daniel, Alexandra Roxo, Ashley Elizabeth, and Lisa-Marie Schneider.

An enormous thanks to my family. I am so grateful for you, Mommy, your love is why I believe in myself today. My sister Moun, you have been a guiding light, I don't know where I would be if it weren't for your support. To my brother Micky for being a fierce critic in the most loving way. My dad, for teaching me that love languages don't always look the same for everyone.

I want to acknowledge my friend Gabriel Marques for making me laugh, hosting me in his home, and always being such a sweet and funny friend when I most needed it. You've been there for me for so many years. A special thanks to Ruby Warrington for your book wisdom, for your compassion and friendship as I embarked on this journey.

Lastly, I want to thank all the incredible people, friends, and teachers I've met on my travels—you are all my teachers.

About the Author

Sah D'Simone is a spiritual guide, meditation teacher, transformational speaker, and bestselling author--leading a heart-based healing movement rooted in tried-and-true techniques, and pioneering a "spiritually sassy" approach in which joy and authenticity illuminate the path to enlightenment.

Born in Brazil, Sah immigrated to the US at age 16. By his early 20s, he had found great success in the fashion industry as co-founder and creative director of an international fashion magazine, and yet he was overwhelmed by addiction, depression, and anxiety. In 2012, he walked away from everything and began an intensive search for health and well-being.

In 2013, Sah embarked on a journey to Nepal, India, Thailand, and Indonesia to study with great spiritual masters like His Holiness the Dalai Lama, Lama Zopa Rinpoche, Jetsunma Tenzin Palmo, and countless others. Sah developed a revolutionary healing approach, blending ancient Tantric Buddhism and modern contemplative pyschotherapy, served with a twist of his trademark sass. He is also passionate about mental health and well-being in the LGBTQIA+ and POC communities.

Sah's teachings have helped enrich the lives of thousands, and he has shared the stage with Deepak Chopra, Yung Pueblo, Ruby Warrington, and Dan Harris. His first book, 5-minute Daily Meditations, is an international bestseller, translated into Spanish, Chinese, and Dutch. He has been invited to speak at TEDx, and his client list includes Google, MoMa, Kanye West, Cannes Lion, American Express, the United Nations, New Balance, Bloomingdales, and Havas.

Learn more about Sah on his website: sahdsimone.com

bout Sounds True

Sounds True is a multimedia publisher whose mission is to inspire and support personal transformation and spiritual awakening. Founded in 1985 and located in Boulder, Colorado, we work with many of the leading spiritual teachers, thinkers, healers, and visionary artists of our time. We strive with every title to preserve the essential "living wisdom" of the author or artist. It is our goal to create products that not only provide information to a reader or listener but also embody the quality of a wisdom transmission.

For those seeking genuine transformation, Sounds True is your trusted partner. At SoundsTrue.com you will find a wealth of free resources to support your journey, including exclusive weekly audio interviews, free downloads, interactive learning tools, and other special savings on all our titles.

To learn more, please visit SoundsTrue.com/freegifts or call us toll-free at 800.333.9185.

sounds true
WAKING UP THE WORLD